THE RN PARADIGM

Andy R

ACKNOWLEDGMENTS

Background cover image: Globular Cluster M10
credit: ESA/Hubble & NASA

Woodland creature artwork
& RN Type icons by Andy R

The RN Paradigm is a work of fiction and is, in many respects, complete nonsense. Names, characters, businesses, places, references, events, books, locales, and incidents are either the products of the author's imagination or used in a fictitious manner. Any resemblance to actual persons, living or dead, existing works or actual events is purely coincidental. Any humor is intentional any offence is not.

Copyright © 2019 Andy R
All rights reserved.
ISBN: 9781096561934

Vik, was that the doorbell?

BUSINESS SURVIVAL

This book is about success.

It's about winning.

It's about understanding that the world is a big complicated machine with lots of moving parts.

It's about making that machine work for you.

There are millions of businesses worldwide destined to fail, not because they lack a good product or service, but because they fail to grasp the fundamental forces of the world in which they operate. If you can understand the business universe, you can avoid failure. This understanding is not easy to come by – if it was, everyone would be successful. However, this understanding can be taught.

Walk into any bookshop and you will find books. Many of those books are about management and success and I've spent decades living and breathing their teachings, applying them to business and expcriencing where those books got it right and more importantly, where they got it wrong.

This book is for those people who, as part of their job, are made to read management guides. But it is also for those who have never read a management guide or for those who are just curious about how to dominate the business world and make more than the GDP of a small country.

Through tireless immersion in the world of finance, business and management I came to realize that the majority of management literature had made the same mistake: they had relied too heavily upon anecdotes and the personal experiences of the author. So I set out to avoid making this mistake.

My journey to enlightenment really began back in 2008. I was having lunch with several thought pioneers and the prevailing view at the time was Nietzsche's maxim "that which does not kill us makes us stronger," but in a chance comment I had flipped this on its head and opined that, "if something is stronger than you, it can always kill you." There were some exchanged looks acknowledging that I had spoken a profound truth. The managing director of a large multinational leaned over and said admiringly, "I'm impressed with your insight, but in itself, this is a worthless observation." Intrigued, I asked him to elaborate and he explained that it's never about a single parameter. The world is far more complicated than that. "No," he said wisely, "it's always two parameters." He was, of course, correct, but whilst he and the others around that table had a sense of this natural order, they had failed to realize that simply understanding that the whole world is governed by just two parameters is not helpful until you know which two.

Why do some businesses succeed and others fail? I have to confess at the time I don't think I fully appreciated the genius of my own insight. In 2012, I was at a winter conference casually discussing my theory with the academic warriors, Richmond and Nillesen. Nillesen, with his sharp suit and quick wit, had been a sensation as the key-note, demolishing long-held orthodoxies with his powerful research and searing criticism. I was naturally flattered that a man of such intellect was taking the time to hear my ideas. Richmond of course, was there in his shorts and t-shirt, carrying his rolled up bathmat and brandishing his infamous ideas-Frisbee. They both excitedly tried to explain how my ideas beautifully simplified their own research; it was the key they had been looking for. I suggested that we work together and even though they insisted we name the resulting theory after me, I wouldn't have it. Sure, the moment of genius was mine, but the hard work of collecting the data and producing the formal mathematical description of my insights was all down to Richmond and Nillesen. The profound insight that had so excited them now seems obvious. In many ways, I suppose I had always known the truth. As do all of us. It's baked into our DNA. Our most basic of survival instincts: fight or flight.

This is not just some abstract idea that is taught at school: it's a fundamental principle woven into the genetic fabric of every animal on the planet. In a critical situation, we respond using our instinct, instincts that have been honed through millions of years of evolution. And whilst the modern city or office environment might appear unrelated to the survival struggles of our distant ancestors, they are not.

What Richmond and Nillesen had realized was that whatever the business, no matter how complicated its mission statement, no matter how disparate its locations, no matter what services it provides or what goods it manufacturers, all businesses are composed of the same thing: people. No matter how hard you try, you can't name a business that wasn't either founded by a person or currently employs people. And those people are subject to the same basic wiring as the rest of us. When you shine those instinctual responses of fight or flight through the prism of a twenty-first-century business, you have the central concepts of the Richmond-Nillesen Paradigm: aggression and speed.

The only difference between a successful business and a failed business is all of their actions and decisions. And time and time again when we go to analyze the poor decisions that have led to market failures, we see a reluctance or an inability to fully appreciate the balance between speed and aggression. What the RN Paradigm teaches us is that when correctly calibrated, the balance between speed and aggression will be the critical factor between being triumphant or being defeated.

The market place is littered with losers. Why did they lose? Often it is not because their products were worse or their management less competent, but because they failed to utilize speed at the right time or because they were not effectively aggressive at the crucial moment. And what do successful businesses show us? They show us that they are consistently applying and re-calibrating their RN Paradigm parameters to suit the opportunities and the risks that they face.

Businesses often tell us the same thing: if we could better capture opportunities and identify risks, we could double our capacity and output. This is worth thinking about – a doubling of capacity and output. Imagine the opportunities that would arise from doubling your output. The application of the RN Paradigm whilst no guarantee of doubling output will allow you to approach opportunities and risks with a speed of response that will amaze your competitors and leave them behind. Applied correctly and calibrated accordingly, it will deliver success and allow for rapid and controlled growth.

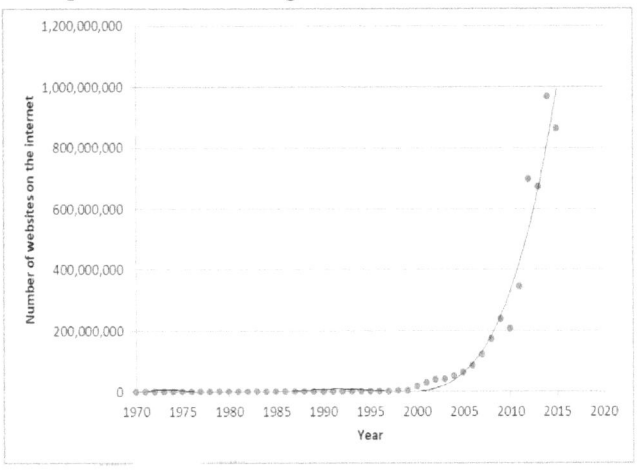

Graph 1 – illustrating that the number of websites only started to increase once the internet was invented. Act fast!

On the surface, the RN Paradigm might look like any other management theory, but this is where you are wrong. Other management guides seek to simplify the inherently complex system of markets and companies down to catchphrases, buzzwords and memorable quotes, and whilst they may be memorable, they are ultimately little more than a collection of observations and anecdotes: stories of what worked in the past for one or two companies. But they cannot be said to be scientific.

Other management guides seek to simplify the inherently complex system of markets and companies down to catchphrases, buzzwords and memorable quotes

---

A scientific model doesn't just look at the past and say what once happened, it seeks to extract the critical components from those events and then construct an overarching, abstracted model that can be employed to predict future events. The reason a scientific model is superior to an anecdotal one is that the scientific method, arguably the most powerful tool humanity has developed for exploring the universe, takes data, fashions a hypothesis and then tests that hypothesis with yet more data. It is easy to assert rules and laws if you don't require them to be refutable. It's important to realize that the RN Paradigm is not constructed from something as fleeting as mere opinion, it is based on the work of a research team of academics who, recognizing the value of my central insights, worked to find the data that confirmed those insights.

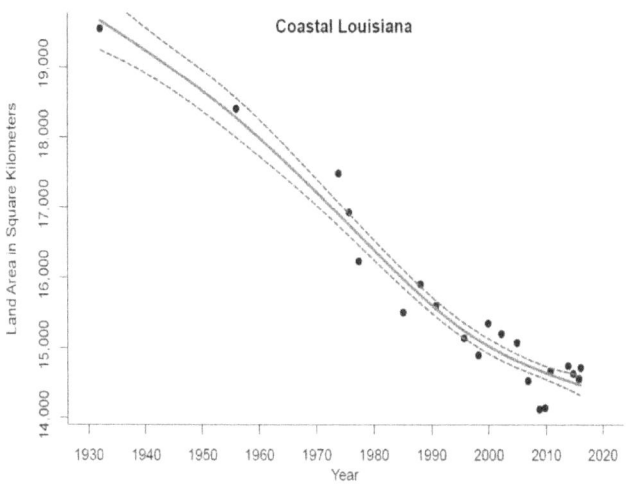

Graph 2 – Loss of land area in Coastal Louisiana demonstrating the effect of relentless aggression by the sea.
Source: USGS (public domain)

Everyone has a talent or two in life, something that they are good at, something that distinguishes them from others, be it golf or math, and if pushed I suppose I'd say mine are humility and transcendent insights into the universe. So whilst successful businesses might be part of a complex system of interlocking factors that seem impossibly confusing to everyone else, one of my profound insights was that the tools for understanding these successes were already within us all. My humility had allowed me to recognize that all of the hard work had already been done by evolution, which is what makes the RN Paradigm so incredibly powerful. The basic ideas of speed and aggression are a natural part of everyday life. The RN Paradigm allows these to be applied to business.

People often ask where I get my insights from and I suspect that many of them come from my experience of being a completely self-made man. When you've dragged yourself up out of poverty by your own bootstraps and fought every inch of the way up the ladder of success, you develop a strong sense of what's possible and as any self-made individual will tell you, you have a much keener perception of those around you and a much greater resilience when you encounter setbacks. I think it's safe to say that I acquired my success entirely through my own efforts. With the possible exceptions of a nationalized education system that educated both me and all of my employees, a structured judiciary, a physical infrastructure of roads and utilities maintained by a succession of stable democratic governments presiding over historically unprecedented levels of national wealth, an international system of finance governed by clear guidelines and the technological, scientific, medical and mathematical contributions of countless individuals whose preceding work was largely funded through public money. With the exception of these, I can comfortably take credit for my own success.

THE PARADIGM

This book does not require the reader to be a manager or to have read anything from the Madrid-Barnsley canon of management. The central concepts of speed and aggression are sufficiently intuitive that they could be explained to a lay audience in a bar as easily as to experts in a lecture theatre: that is a part of their beauty. In the same way that Einstein's theory of relativity can be simplified down to produce Newtonian mechanics, so too can the Richmond-Nillesen Paradigm be simplified down to explain the majority of traditional management styles. This book introduces the principles of speed and aggression and then explores the subsequent simplification of the RN equations.

WHO'S IN THE DRIVING SEAT?

Events within a business are part of the real world and as such, that business is subject to the randomness and chaotic nature of reality. Even a well-defined business in a well-understood market is better thought of as a series of complex inter-competing forces. The decisions or actions that make one business successful can, under a different set of external restrictions, be the breaking of that business. Given that the success of a business is so critically dependent upon its context and individual circumstances it is almost nonsensical to generalize a series of steps or rules that should be applied. A sharp-minded businessman would already be wary of such quick-fix solutions, knowing that success is more than just a paint-by-numbers affair. If a series of rules was all it took to produce a successful business then there would be one manual, everybody would use it and everybody would be successful. Since we don't see universal success it is probably safe to assume that a simple series of universal rules are of little help.

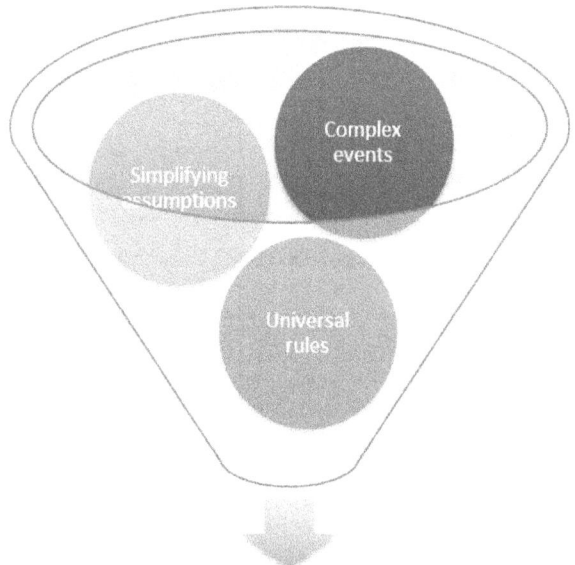

Unhelpful solution?

However, if science teaches us one thing it's that a simple model can be built upon to make a more robust, complex model that can be made to work for us. In getting men to the moon the lunar capsule was modelled as though it was a point mass, a mass with no volume, a single point in space.

Planet Earth is blue and there's nothing I can do

Now obviously the lunar module isn't a single point in space because people were placed inside the module, but this simple idea, that it was a point, was built on and made more complex when it was needed. Likewise, a business can adapt a simple model and make it fit their context.

TEACHING THROUGH PARABLES

"Why does it have to be so complicated?" That was the feedback we kept getting in the early days of developing the RN Paradigm. Businesses were hungry for that multi-million dollar success, but not if it was going to be complicated. They wanted simple ideas that could be expressed in a single word or less: ideas like 'innovate' or 'speed'. So when they were presented with the scientifically balanced RN Paradigm and all its myriad complexities, they were overwhelmed. Richmond, who developed many of the mathematical structures necessary to reconcile the velocity-eigenstates within an orthogonal aggression-space construct, believed that whilst the RN Paradigm was powerfully complex, it was possible to explain its central ideas to a lay audience.

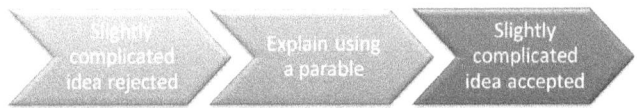

Chichester Chevron Methodology (1935)

He suggested using parables to teach the four limiting conditions of the speed and aggression parameters, citing the success of the Chichester Chevron Methodology (CCM) that was so popular in the inter-war period. Richmond's parables have since become famous the world over for their stunning simplicity, heart-warming characters and the powerful enlightenment they invite. The parables have thus been included throughout the following sections.

Many of the woodland creatures that feature in the parables are available as soft toys that can be purchased through the website.

AGGRESSION

Aggression is usually understood to be a negative term and there are good reasons for this. We may speak of an aggressive expansion or an aggressive colleague or an aggressive takeover but in order to appreciate the term, we need to unpack what is being expressed and who is doing that expression.

THE PARABLE OF NOT HAVING ENOUGH AGGRESSION

Flappy the owl sat on a low branch of the oak tree and tapped the bark to get everyone's attention. The other woodland animals all quietened down to hear what Flappy had to say.

"I've called this meeting because we're all worried about the lions." There was a murmur of agreement amongst the gathered creatures. "The lions have been taking over more and more of the forest and something needs to be done," Flappy said.

Speedy the rabbit spoke up. "I say we run away," he said and with that he hopped away.

Flappy the owl shook his head. "I don't think we should run away. I think we should talk with the lions and make them realize that they already have enough territory and don't need any more."

Virile the bull stamped his foot. "I disagree. I don't think we should be talking with them. Lions shouldn't even be in a forest, this isn't their natural habitat. We should stand up to the lions. We should kill them on sight." A few of the other animals agreed with Virile the Bull but Flappy the owl seemed uncertain.

"But what if we make them angry?" Flappy said. "I think we should negotiate. Make them see reason."

From the other side of the clearing three lions appeared and approached the group of gathered animals. Flappy the owl flapped over to them. "We want to talk with you about how you've been taking over the forest. We'd like you to stop."

The head lion blinked at Flappy. "Why would we stop?" he said. "You're all too weak to stop us so we're just going to carry on." And with that, the three lions pounced on Flappy who died in a cloud of feathers.

"Oh no," the woodland creatures said. "Flappy is dead. What shall we do now?"

Diagram 17 – Flappy the owl

Virile the bull stamped his foot and charged at the lions. The lions looked surprised that someone was fighting back and tried to attack Virile the bull, but his aggression was too much for them and he overpowered and killed two of the lions. The head lion held up a paw. "Stop," he said. Virile stood facing the head lion. "You're a strong fighter," the head lion said. "And we respect that. We will leave this forest forever and return to our natural habitat." And so, the head lion walked out of the forest and back to the savannah where he found and ate Speedy, the rabbit who had run away.

The woodland creatures cheered. "Your aggression protected us by scaring off the lions," they said.

"Yes," said Virile the bull. "It did."

And to this day you don't find lions in forests.

AGGRESSION IN RELATIONSHIPS IS BAD

If one speaks of an aggressive act they are really calling attention to a power imbalance and it is almost always being highlighted by the disenfranchised. There are some good reasons why we might think of aggression as being a negative trait. In personal relationships aggression is not only harmful and undesirable but it ceases to show strength and is almost always an indication of weakness: one who shouts and bellows at their partner never commands respect. We see them as a pathetic, impotent figure. But this is the problem. Too many well-meaning businessmen carry this negative idea of aggression from the world of personal relationships and carry it through into the world of business relationships.

AGGRESSION IN BUSINESS IS GOOD

But the world of business is not the world of personal relationships. In business when someone describes a negotiator as aggressive, what they are describing is a strong negotiator who is in control. What they are expressing is their dismay at not being in that strong position. An aggressive position in business is simply a strong position that is being described by the weaker party. From the perspective of the aggressor their position is no more aggressive than their breakfast was, it is simply the strong position that they have chosen to occupy.

A strong position, however, is not possible without self-belief. You must know that what you're doing is correct. There are many self-help guides that can help try and boost your confidence but if you're plotting a course for greatness you won't have time for that. The simplest way to improve the strength of your position is to be proven right over and over again and to work your way around the Hexagon of Confidence. That way, as your business ascends, so too will your self-belief. Your ego will become one with your business and thus failure no longer becomes an option, because failure now implies the cataclysmic implosion of your identity.

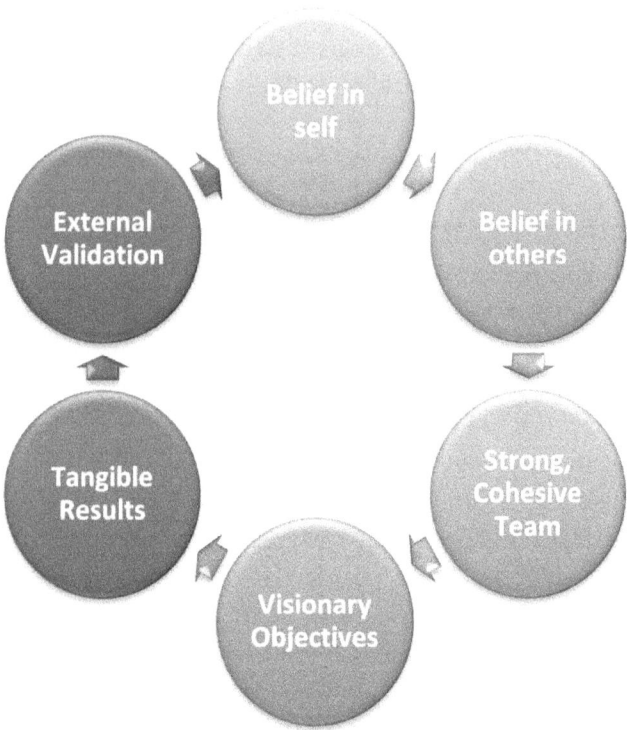

Hexagon of Confidence (Nillesen & Richmond 2011)

A strong, confident manager is able to make the game-changing decisions needed to take a business onto the next level. But a manager can't be aggressive if they're not confident and confidence, as the Hexagon shows us, is ultimately about making the right decisions and reaping the rewards of those decisions. If you are constantly making bad decisions then those around you will lose confidence in your ability and you will lose confidence in yourself.

The more astute amongst you will recognize that the Hexagon is just a six-fold diagrammatic reframing of the familiar Connelly equation

$$S^V + T = R$$

S = Self-belief   V = Validation   T = Teamwork
R = results.

And as any second-year management-theory student can tell you: when rearranged, Connelly describes the conditions necessary for generating self-belief.

$$(R - T)^{\frac{1}{V}} = S$$

Self-belief is thus a simple case of subtracting teamwork from the results and then raising this to the reciprocal power of validation. Or put another way, people are more likely to view your decisions positively if you're making the right choices.

WHEN TO ACT

The choice of when to act aggressively is critical. Generally speaking, if resources are scarce, that is the market is a **thin market,** there will be increased competition for those limited resources. In a thin market, the business is usually best served with an aggressive stance, although the opposite can also be true. Control of limited resources always gives the business a significant advantage over its competitors and will facilitate an improved market position and increased corporate momentum as a result. This is summarized in diagram 7a. Notice how this arrow is pointing upwards: this is good.

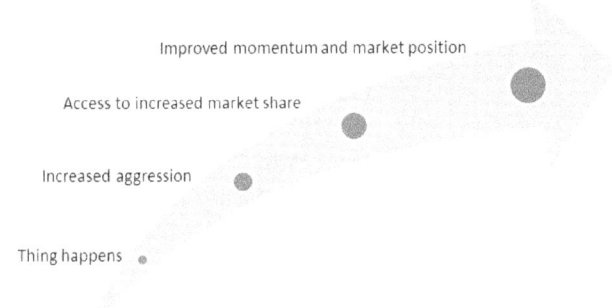

Diagram 7a

If resources are relatively abundant, then we can describe the business as operating within a **thick market**. In a thick market, an aggressive stance is usually the most beneficial position for the business to take, although, there are obviously examples where the opposite can be true. Thick markets are characterized by diverse competition wherein consumers' needs can be met by multiple niche businesses.

If you're already established within a thick market then an aggressive stance might seem vital since it will maintain the status quo and demonstrate to your competitors that you are in a strong position. This is often true. However, we must remember Sun Tsu's advice from The Art of War to *"appear weak when you are strong, and strong when you are weak."*

Appear weak when you are strong, and strong when you are weak.

Thus, when you are in a strong position the aggressive stance might be to appear weak! It might seem counter-intuitive, but ask any CEO of any highly successful business from the last century and they will have heard of Sun Tsu's Art of War. Some businesses actively cite Sun Tsu's teachings in their strategy. Why? Because business is a battlefield and Sun Tsu is a wise general. You might argue that this doesn't address the core argument of why appearing weak would be a viable business strategy, or indeed why we are even looking at ancient Chinese texts to glean an understanding of modern business methodology and in some ways you would be correct. But are we to hubristically imagine that we know more about twenty-first-century business than a Chinese general from 2500 years ago? Think about it: Sun Tsu never had one of his multi-nationals fail. Thus, in a thick market, the strong business should not advertise its strength.

However, if you are breaking into a thick market from a position of weakness and if we assume that the advice of an Iron Age Chinese general is correct, then an obviously aggressive stance is essential. With an abundance of resources and a surfeit of competition, the market is unlikely to hold that many strong actors and thus acting with aggression may convince others that your strategy is working – even if it isn't. Remember, confidence unlocks aggression and once you have confidence in your business plans (because they've been shown to work) then your aggression will bring rewards. Again Sun Tsu states that *"opportunities multiply as they are seized."*

Opportunities multiply as they are seized

So for the small, niche competitor, an aggressive stance is to expand and occupying several niche competitors and thus slowly gain market dominance. Unless of course, this drains vital resources from your core business, then it's a bad idea.

There is, of course, an obvious problem with Sun Tsu's advice: if appearing weak when you are strong and strong when you are weak was a winning strategy, everybody would do it and the advantage would evaporate. So really, Sun Tsu is advocating the promotion of uncertainty and then seizing upon that uncertainty to leverage an advantage. If your competitors and potential customers are slow-witted and lack reliable information about your business, then it is possible to gain a measure of success through sheer bluster and deception. If however, your competitors and customers are intelligent and they have access to good information, then you are restricted to becoming successful through the merits of your business.

THE AGGRESSION ANOMALY

Early on in our testing, customers would argue that it looked like aggression was the correct stance in all situations, since it applies to both established entities and start-ups, and in both thick markets and thin markets. This misunderstanding is called the aggression anomaly and it fails to appreciate what the paradigm is describing. It is impossible for a business to reduce its aggression (or its velocity) to zero and as such, a business will always have some non-zero quantity in each parameter. For every situation a business encounters, there are a particular set of aggression-velocity values that will generate success (the particular definition of success is quite important here and is usually encoded in the specific business tensor). Since each situation is located on a continuous timeline of events, we can use the Borsuk-Ulam theorem to conclude that there will be a continuum of aggression values that will perfectly resolve every situation – assuming the correct economic curvature for the business in question. Thus, whenever a business is successful it will necessarily have had some aggression value but this does not mean that the aggression value was solely responsible for that success any more than the ambient temperature was. However, the aggression coupled with the velocity and a detailed understanding of the business does give us an insight into that success. It's worth noting that the RN equations also allow for a negative solution wherein a business is able to position their aggression-velocity values to provide them with a continuous stream of the worst possible outcomes. Try and avoid this.

THE PARABLE OF HAVING TOO MUCH AGGRESSION

Angry the hedgehog walked his usual route through the woods. As he strolled past the squirrels, Angry eyed them menacingly. The squirrels bowed their heads and carried on burying acorns in the dirt; they were behaving themselves because they knew about Angry's legendary aggression. Angry had an important job: he kept the woodland operating efficiently and if there were any problems that needed sorting, Angry would sort them out. Without him, Angry was sure the place would fall apart.

Frantic the ferret ran up to Angry. "Come quick!" he exclaimed, bouncing up and down. "There's a thing... it's a thing, I don't know what it is."

Angry puffed up his chest and strode steadily after Frantic. About an hour later, Frantic the ferret rushed up to Sensible the vixen. "It's Angry," he said bouncing up and down. "It's a massive fight, massive. You gotta come see." Sensible followed Frantic to a clearing where Angry was repeatedly punching a concrete pillar. Sensible walked over.

"What are you doing?" she asked.

"I won't let it defeat me," Angry bellowed. "I will make it respect me."

Sensible looked at the concrete pillar and the patch of blood that Angry was punching. "It's a concrete pillar, Angry. Can you not see that your absurdly elevated aggression is causing you to attack something that is in no way a threat?"

Angry shook his head and slammed his right fist against the unrelenting surface. "I wouldn't expect someone like you to understand," Angry said, sneering at Sensible. "It's about commanding respect, you see. The woodland respects me. They see how strong I am." He slammed his left fist into the concrete. "And this right here is disrespectful."

Diagram 11 – Angry the hedgehog

"It's a concrete pillar. I fail to see how that's disrespectful."

"I asked it a straightforward question and it chose to ignore me. Now that was its choice and it's experiencing the consequences." Angry punched the concrete again. "Look. Look at how powerful I am. I'm defeating this enemy. I'm strong and powerful."

Sensible shook her head. "No, Angry. No, you are none of those things. No one respects you because you're an imbecile who attacks inanimate objects in the deluded belief that it shows you to be strong."

"Ha, that's where you're wrong, see. I am strong. Look, I'm winning." Angry shouted. "You know how I know I'm winning? Because I'm repeatedly punching my opponent in the face."

Sensible shook her head. "That makes no sense, Angry; you have too much aggression." She said and walked away. Angry continued to punch the concrete block for a further three days. By the third day, Angry had grown too weak to defend himself and was eaten by a passing dog. The woodland immediately became a happier, more productive place.

ACCELERATION

A market is not like some natural resource that can be mined or cultivated and that market cannot simply be seized from your competitors like some medieval kingdom. The market is an abstract idea: it is the coordinated needs and purchasing desires of your potential customers and as such, it can be created, grown or destroyed by your products and services. An aggressive strategy can be one that either seeks to protect existing markets or one that seeks to find new ones, but in either case, if the business is to adapt to their success they will need to change their velocity. In business, we call this concept of changing velocity, acceleration. Perhaps the easiest way to picture this new "acceleration" concept is to imagine the business as a car. Now imagine that car is changing its velocity, either getting faster and faster or slower and slower: this is analogous to acceleration.

In a thick market, that is one filled with many potential customers, too much aggression focused towards one outcome can have the effect of increasing inertia. An increase in inertia reduces acceleration and makes it harder for the business to change direction. What at first glance may have looked like a strong, positive position can suddenly be revealed to be a slow, lumbering position that renders it incapable of reacting to a change in that market. This is highlighted in diagram 8b. Notice that the arrow is pointing down this time. This is bad.

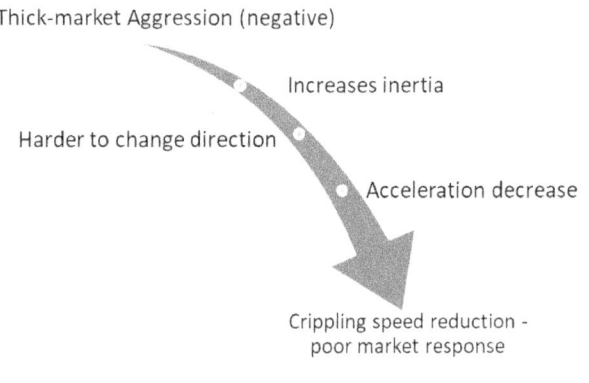

Diagram 8b

THE LITIGATION STRATEGY

Occasionally, customers ask us to explain existing business strategies within the framework of the RN Paradigm. Of course, when certain parameters are constrained, many of these strategies drop out as solutions to the RN equations. One of the solutions is the litigation strategy and is highly recommended by many leading law firms. Here, a business that is already in a strong position (or one that wishes to just appear strong) adopts an aggressive strategy of litigating at every opportunity. There are several advantages to this strategy beyond simply enriching your lawyers. The first is the drag factor it can inflict upon competitors. An increased drag will reduce their velocity and can prevent them from reaching new markets or reacting rapidly enough to secure new customers. It can also reduce the aggression of your competitors, making them think twice before infringing patent rights, or embarking upon litigation of their own. Aggressive litigation can also have a suppressive effect on start-ups, with spurious infringement suits stifling their growth and tending to produce a more cautious low-aggression approach, both of which can improve your market share.

There are some downsides. Extensive litigation is costly and in the extreme, the strategy becomes similar to taking out new loans to pay off old ones. However, with the loan analogy, there is arguably a tipping point where the size of the loan becomes sufficiently large that the lending bank cannot afford for you to default and the debtor is to some extent protected. But with litigation, there is no known limit that a business can incur and that lawyers are not prepared to pursue. Thus litigation can bankrupt a business long before it accrues the benefit of any increased revenues. For this strategy to work long term, a business needs to maintain substantial velocity: attention must be continually redirected to increasingly new and shiny projects to entice each new wave of investors. And with each new wave of investment, it is imperative that you continue to project success and press forward with desperate litigation to suppress the rumors about any earlier failures. This strategy, commonly known as the Dump Polygon, emerges from the RN equations as a closed market loop, however, the constant acceleration required to maintain the loop inevitably radiates capital costs in a process called *synchrotron decapitalization*. The loop can initially appear to be successful but the increasing loss of velocity usually results in indictments for running a Ponzi scheme.

The Dump Polygon (Miller et al)

THE AGGRESSION SINGULARITY

The RN equations predict that when a large business engages in a sufficiently aggressive strategy it is possible for that business to warp the economic curvature of its connected markets to such an extent that those competing too closely will find themselves torn apart by the extreme economic forces. Small, low-mass start-ups are sometimes able to compete successfully in these markets by adopting extremely high-velocities but they always run the risk of getting too close and losing all their resources. Once a business reaches this critical point of aggression, all of its projects become extensions of the central aggression singularity and its velocity drops to a minimum. This might seem like an ideal position, but there is a downside. Having consumed its local markets and lacking the velocity to adapt and move to new markets, the business continues to radiate capital costs and will eventually evaporate into bankruptcy. This is not through any fault of the business, indeed, all actions beyond this critical point are futile and will only hasten the inevitable by radiating more capital costs. There is no escaping the central bankruptcy. This is just the way of things.

SPEED

One business might choose an aggressive stance to secure their resources but the competition doesn't always have to play the same game. Aggressive competition can drain resources and sometimes those resources are best placed in promoting speed, which might be realized by regularly switching resource suppliers and negotiating lower costs or through innovation and the development of new markets.

THE PARABLE OF NOT ENOUGH SPEED

Largo the Rabbit sat in the woodland clearing enjoying the warmth of the sun on his nose. From out of the woods bounded Largo's best friend, Speedy.

"Hey Speedy," Largo said. "How's it going?"

"I'm worried," Speedy said, looking over his shoulder. "I think we need to move out of the forest as soon as we can."

"Why would we leave the forest?" Largo said. "We've always lived in the forest; the forest provides us with everything we need."

"Things are going to change around here."

Largo laughed. "People are always saying things are going to change. Remember when the river dried up and everyone said we were doomed? " Largo said.

Speedy nodded. "Well look what happened. We were all fine, right? The river had just shifted its course."

Speedy shook his head. "I think this time it's different. You remember how the great wall began to appear around the same time as the river dried up?"

Largo laughed. "A wall is just a wall. It can't do anything to us."

Speedy shrugged. "I don't know, Largo. I think the great wall might be a part of a large hydroelectric project and that this entire valley will be flooded to produce a reservoir and that you and everyone you love will drown because you weren't quick enough to respond to the evidence that things were changing."

"Nonsense," Largo said. "The forest has always supported us, why would it suddenly stop doing that?"

"Because it will be under 200metres of water."

"I don't believe you," Largo said shaking his head. "Look how lovely and warm and sunny it is. We're not drowning right now, so how could we possibly drown in the future? You're an idiot Speedy: you're just running away from your own fear."

"No, I'm running away from the water that will inevitably drown you and your refusal to accept change. Your argument is based on inductive reasoning and the assumption that the past will be like the future."

Largo shrugged. "Fine, run away if you want to, Speedy. You're wasting your energy though."

Speedy ran up the side of the valley telling the other creatures about the hydroelectric scheme. The next day the valley was flooded and Largo was dead.

Diagram 13 – Speedy the rabbit

MOVE FAST, MOVE FIRST

Nowadays companies that specialize in trading on the markets are competing to be housed next to where the stock market is physically based. This may seem surprising in a world which is interconnected and where, with the help of a laptop and Wi-Fi, work can be done from anywhere at any time. Yet information still needs to travel through the cables connected to the computer giving the information. The difference in being right next to the server or further away may be nanoseconds but this time is an advantage. *"In the age of high-frequency trading, technological speed itself is a strategy,"* Benjamin Van Vliet (Illinois Institute of Technology's Stuart School of Business). In the early days of computer trading companies would position their computers as close to the stock exchange as they could to gain that time advantage. The New York stock exchange now ensures that each server rack is fed information through the same lengths of cable, thus removing the advantage of physical location. However, there are still advantages to be had in having the shortest distance between exchanges, like New York and Chicago. Mountains were bored through to ensure that companies could gain a few microseconds over their competitors. Their aggressive approach to being the fastest, even by a few nanoseconds, meant they could outperform their competitors.

THE CONSTANT NEED FOR MOVEMENT

To be stationary is to be dead. A shark must keep swimming or it will drown. A business must keep on improving otherwise it too will die. A company making typewriters in the first half of the last century might well imagine itself to be too big to fail; they've been hugely successful, they're a household name and they have numerous factories with a expanding market. The company made its money manufacturing typewriters and so it sees no reason to deviate from this winning formula. What worked yesterday will surely continue to work tomorrow. This inductive reasoning is common amongst the larger companies for the simple reason that they've already got the winning formula. Why run the risk of trying something new when you're already a huge, successful company? And inevitably the typewriter companies fade away to become little more than a cautionary tale in a management guide. But the smaller startup, the company with little to lose will end up being the nimble successor that picks up on the desktop computer and supersedes the ponderous giants of the past. (It is also true that there are small startups that make bad decisions, but their disappearance is only important when trying to explain the concept of survivor bias).

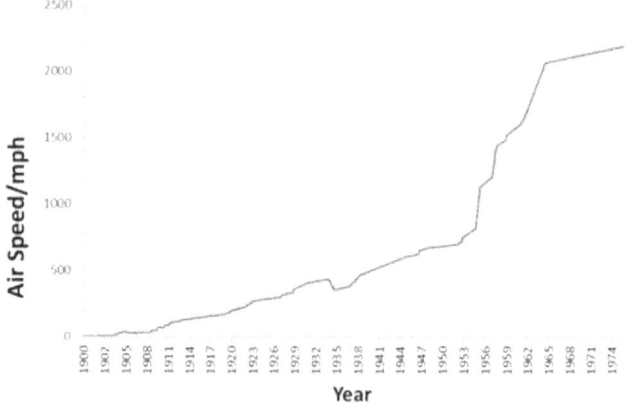

Graph 3 – illustrating that the speed of planes has increased with time. Be fast!

It's important to adapt and to change and to stay nimble because markets are always changing along with the technologies that drive them. But there's a danger in telling ourselves the story of the successful behemoth whose refusal to innovate led to their demise because it's only part of the story. Yes, it's important to change, but what does that look like? If you're someone like Coca Cola and you have a highly successful recipe, what does constant motion look like? If you read the cautionary tale of the typewriter and are inspired by the need to constantly innovate, are you going to burst into the next board meeting of Coca Cola, slam your hands on the desk and say they need to phase out Coke? Assuming, of course, you're employed by Coca Cola, otherwise, the outcome is predictably being escorted from the building. But what lesson is Coca Cola supposed to draw from the tale of the typewriter? Is the lesson one of needing to constantly innovate and if so what does innovation look like in their market? Is it to expand the product lines and reach new markets? Or is it to consolidate the market you have and come up with a new advertising campaign? The problem is, there isn't a single answer and there certainly isn't an answer that can be drawn from an anecdote. All the cautionary tale of the typewriter really tells you, is that if you're making typewriters in the latter half of the twentieth century you need to switch your product line. It doesn't tell you anything about your current market or how to adapt within it.

That's not to say the tale has no utility. Of course it does. Being aware of how things went wrong in the past is arguably a good indicator of how they might go wrong in the future. The danger is in over-interpretation.

INERTIA

One of the main difficulties an organization faces in implementing a speed strategy is in reducing their inertia. Employees settle into routines and management relaxes into the familiar. During normal operation, these conditions are important as they provide stability and opportunities to improve efficiencies. However, when pursuing a high-velocity strategy, these comforts are the very inertia that inhibits change: they slow the organization down. The task that faces a good manager is in reducing inertia without destabilizing staff infrastructure. It's worth looking back at the classic Change Inequality (Gleicher, Beckhard, Harris) to get a handle on how we can achieve this.

$$D \times V \times F > R$$

D= Dissatisfaction V= Vision F= First steps
R= Resistance to change (Ω) x = multiplied by
>= inequality symbol for greater than

Thus, staff can be motivated into overcoming their innate resistance through a combination of an inspiring vision, increasing their dissatisfaction or instigating the first steps of the change you wish to see. Which of these variables you choose to prioritize will depend on the strategy you are seeking to implement and there are numerous guides dedicated to each of the variables and discussing the pros and cons of how they play out in a market setting. Broadly speaking the Vienna Gambit prioritizes dissatisfaction; the Etruscan Spread, vision and the Kolmogorov Stance, the first steps.

During the optimization stage of the RN Paradigm, we found that in a high-velocity regime the resistance to change was better approximated by Van Neumann's inequality.

$$\left(D^{\frac{3}{2}} \times V \times F^2\right)\gamma > R$$

Where γ is obviously the Lorentz factor. This suggests that the Kolmogorov Stance is likely to be a more efficient choice when the paradigm calls for an increase in speed.

THE VELOCITY ILLUSION

There are times where a company needs to move rapidly and the faster they move the greater the benefit. The economy might suddenly take a downturn and extraneous assets need to be liquidated or maybe a new technology suddenly opens up a whole new marketplace and you're amongst the first to respond. At these points the faster your company can react, the greater the benefit, but these occasions are few and they are temporary. When companies respond rapidly they can reap huge rewards and this can lead them into a high-velocity strategy, constantly driving their company after new markets. But high velocity comes at a price. It's heavy on resources and it's heavy on your staff. A cheetah does not run at 70mph all day, it only breaks out its top speed when it absolutely has to. Why? Because running at 70mph takes an extraordinary amount of energy and if there's no pay off at the end, the cheetah will eventually die. The mistake that is often made is to assume that the high velocity creates the benefit. It does not. The high velocity enables the company to retrieve the benefit before others, but the benefit is externally generated. Thus, velocity does not generate the destination. Under the RN Paradigm, this is known as the Velocity Illusion.

Velocity does not generate the destination.

It might seem obvious but it is surprising how often people and organizations succumb to the Velocity Illusion. Sustained high velocity actually has the counter-intuitive effect of increasing inertia. A group that tries to constantly break new markets will ultimately be directing resources away from developing the markets it has just acquired. In the office environment the Velocity Illusion is often observed through staff being pressured to meet constantly shifting targets. Targets may well be reached by the staff immolating themselves, working all hours and forgoing their home lives, because as we all know, a shark will die if it stops swimming.

However, we have also seen that a cheetah dies when it keeps on sprinting. This leads us to an important adjunct to the Velocity Illusion that constant innovation does not create high velocity.

And of course the converse is equally true: rapidly changing things does not mean that your business is being innovative.

Constant innovation does not create high velocity.

This is a particular problem for middle managers who, upon acquiring a new department, often wish to appear innovative and effective and will do so by 'shaking things up'. Unfortunately, lacking either imagination or sometimes intelligence, they will often apply interventions that have no evidential basis for their long term efficacy. Like the **Career Traveler** (see types), they will often have moved on to another department or job before their damage is fully realized. These haphazard interventions are a surefire way to trigger Baker's Diamond of Despair (1995) and whilst there is plenty of literature on how to break the Diamond, the required restructuring still takes resources that could otherwise be employed in gaining market traction.

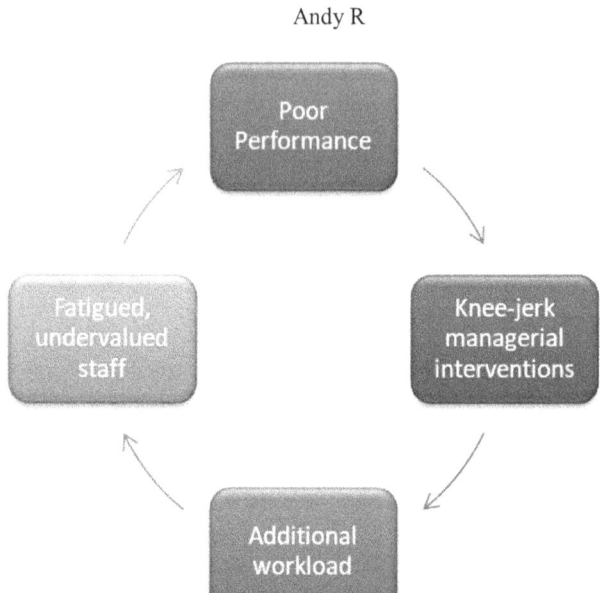

Baker's Diamond of Despair (1995)

So whilst an organization must be prepared to innovate so that, like the shark, it can keep moving and avoid death, it must do so intelligently. Constant movement does not mean constant sprinting. The velocity produced by working on innovations is often velocity enough. The best way for an organization to avoid the Velocity Illusion is education. Senior managers trained in the RN Paradigm are far less likely to succumb to the Velocity Illusion themselves and they will certainly be more skeptical when their subordinates try to present their multiple, unnecessary interventions as innovation. One of the first steps to success is thus training your management in the RN Paradigm.

THE PARABLE OF TOO MUCH SPEED

Martha the Dormouse was moving house and she asked some of her friends whether they could help carry her things across the mountains and the forest to her new home.

"My friend Helen will be there to help you unpack when you arrive, she'll be in all day," Martha said.

Barry the Badger loaded up his car with some of Martha's possessions and settled into the drive. The mountain pass was long and winding and the forest on the other side was huge. Barry knew that there would be no gas stations in between, but he'd done some calculations and concluded that driving at a steady and efficient speed of 50mph would leave him with enough fuel to comfortably make the journey. There was no rush. Barry drove steadily, listening to the teach-yourself-Italian lessons that he had saved on his phone.

Zippy the weasel frantically stuffed Martha's possessions into his car.

"It's a long way," Martha said to Zippy, aware that he had a tendency to do things far too quickly.

"Yeah, yeah, yeah," Zippy said. "It's not that far. I'm gonna drive super, super fast, that'll make the distance way, way shorter."

"That's not how distances work," Martha said. But Zippy didn't listen and jumped into his car. First, Zippy drove across town to get some food. Then he drove back to his house to drop off the extra milk he'd bought. Then he drove round to Rachel Rabbit's place and did a few doughnuts on the road outside her house in a bid to impress her. For some reason, Rachel was not impressed by a weasel laying down strips of rubber in a fully-loaded car with some stranger's drawers strapped to its roof, so Zippy decided to drive to Martha's. Zippy sped off, pushing the car up to its top speed, determined to make the journey as short as possible. The engine screamed as its revs were pushed into the red zone. Three hours later and Zippy shot past Barry the Badger who was still steadily driving along at 50mph. Zippy laughed at him. What a fool.

Diagram 23b – Zippy the weasel

150miles later and Zippy's car had run out of fuel. The car drifted to a stop by the side of the road and Zippy was confused as to what had happened. He had driven fast. He had been the fastest person on the road by far. How could he not have reached his destination? A high velocity always meant you got to your destination faster. He did not understand. Two hours later and Barry the Badger drove past Zippy. Barry still had quite a bit of fuel left and he waved cheerfully at Zippy who was still confused as to why he wasn't at his destination. Barry arrived at Martha's new house, fluent in Italian. Helen asked after Zippy.

"He ran out of fuel on the way," Barry said. "He had too much speed."

Helen looked worried. "That's not good: there are wolves in the forest."

Zippy did not make it through the night.

SPEED TRAPS

When pursuing speed strategies the most important prerequisite is good information. Aggression strategies can endure a certain amount of vagueness around the market conditions but a business that chooses to move quickly and yet has no sense of their context will almost certainly end up in trouble. The very speed that can place you ahead of your competitors can equally place you behind them and the faster you go the greater that effect. Thus, knowledge is crucial. As the Iron Age general says:

Victorious warriors win first and then go to war, while defeated warriors go to war first and then seek to win.

Sun Tsu is not referring to management or business here, but nevertheless we can interpret his words to provide the meaning we want, which in this case is: victory is essential. There's no point in going to war unless you are already victorious and clearly the best way to already be victorious is to define what victory means after the fact.

So why do so many businesses struggle with speed strategies? It's often very simple: to operate at speed, you need wise management who understand the data. Recall that in Whittaker's Onion of Opportunity, the second layer is that of an informed staff. An informed staff is crucial if they are to effectively utilize the infrastructure beneath them.

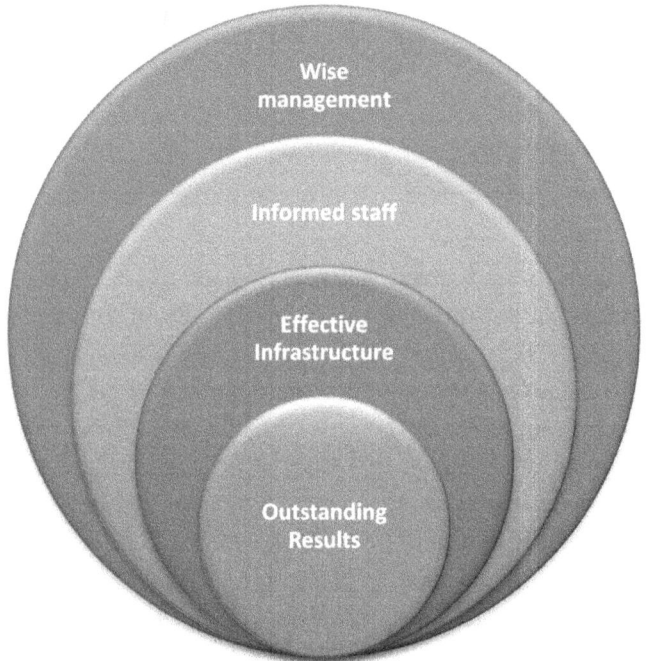

Whittaker's Onion of Opportunity (1972)

Thus in employing a speed strategy, and keeping in mind your Onion, your staff must be given the best information for them to accomplish greatness. But in order to hand down the best information, your management must understand the data, be it about the market or a department's performance. Almost all of the problems we see in speed strategies arise not from the strategies themselves, but in their misapplication, in the data being misunderstood and the wrong strategy being employed. The breakdown is often in the first layer of the onion. We see a lack of speed-wisdom in the management. In comparison, aggression strategies are simple: you always act; it's just a question of how hard. But with speed strategies, the difficulty is in having the wisdom to know when **not** to act because this can be as important, if not more important, than knowing **when** to act. This balance of carefully considered action and inaction requires intelligence, wisdom and the right team of people beneath you.

Remember Sun Tsu's advice from the Art of War is to *"be extremely subtle, even to the point of formlessness. Be extremely mysterious, even to the point of soundlessness. Thereby you can be the director of the opponent's fate."*

Be extremely subtle, even to the point of formlessness. Be extremely mysterious, even to the point of soundlessness. Thereby you can be the director of the opponent's fate.

You will undoubtedly have witnessed that truly excellent managers have the ability to appear mysterious and formless. Those employees who don't understand great management will usually mistake the rambling, unrelated proclamations of their superiors to be the product of ignorance and/or narcissism. But the truly excellent manager is a master of the light touch and is thus able to move with great rapidity. Whilst this ability is obviously vital, this book will not spend a lot of time on this topic as the majority of contemporary management guides already explain how you can be subtle to the point of formlessness and mysterious to the point of soundlessness.

APPLICATION OF THE PARADIGM

The full paradigm is, of course, an elegant and beautiful encapsulation of economics and business and fully describes the topological realm of all possible management operations. Many of the standard management actions will seem obvious when parsed through the lexicon of speed and aggression, but there are some that will not. These are discussed below.

RUNNING THE WRONG WAY UP AN ESCALATOR: NEUTRAL ACTIONS

As all good managers know, there are changes you can make that can give the appearance of an action but without any of the attendant consequences that can wind up making you look good or bad. These are called neutral actions and many management guides have dedicated their entire output to the description of neutral actions.

A good example of a neutral action would be Chen's Lexical Realignment Regime which was made popular in the global bestseller *How to Obliterate the Competition and Avoid Compromise (1996).* The regime, first described in her 1994 book *Prisoner of Your Preconceptions,* began as a serious consideration on how to improve societal well-being through private enterprise.

> *The first step to improving corporate morale is to reduce inequality. Limit your top paid employees to a multiple of your lowest paid. Thus, success at the bottom supports success at the top. This structure will encourage oversight and improve the quality of applicants for productive roles.*
>
> *Pay assigns the worth an organization places on an employee. But pay should not eclipse the smaller details, which in concert with pay, communicate the value you place on their role. A carefully considered job title projects the perceived worth of an employee to the outside world. (1994)*

However, in her bestselling *How to Obliterate the Competition and Avoid Compromise (1996)*, Chen had dropped her initial proposal for improving the pay of employees and simply kept her suggestion of renaming roles. Whilst the realignment was originally intended to provide an inexpensive way for an organization to show that they valued employees, its popularity meant it rapidly showed nothing of the sort. With this collapse in meaning, Lexical Realignment became a popular way for agile managers to appear mysterious in methodology and formless in utility.

Formless management dedicated to the appearance of doing something whilst having no discernable productive output beyond that of continued employment is described under the RN Paradigm as a coordinate transform that preserves both speed and aggression under rotation in the complex plane.

Ex-employees	→ *Part of the extended family*
Receptionist	→*First impressions specialist*
Janitor	→ *Custodial engineer*
Cleaner	→ *Sanitation technician*
Cashier	→ *Financial transaction administrator*
File room gopher	→ *Executor of archived assets*
Mailroom gopher	→ *Executor of commercial correspondence*

Summary of Chen's Lexical Realignment Regime (1996) from Goodwin's Management Compendium (2012)

MAGIC 8-BALL MANAGEMENT

Some managers like to assert their authority by shrouding their decision-making process in mystery. They will often offer cryptic or unhelpful responses such as outlook not so good, ask again later or signs point to yes. This is known as Magic 8-Ball management because it is functionally indistinguishable from using a Magic 8-Ball. Due to its stochastic nature, Magic 8-ball management has no net aggression or velocity: the occasions where it randomly yields positive results will, on a sufficiently long timescale, be balanced by the negatives.

Andy R

EFFECTIVE MANAGEMENT

When we first began exploring the RN Paradigm, our aim was to establish the most effective management style because we assumed that this would be the most popular and profitable information. Despite larger data sets, improved modelling and the development of a quasi-sentient machine-learning algorithm that now only responds to the title Lord Kronos, the model repeatedly concluded that the more time a manager spent facilitating their team, the more effective they would become. However, our early focus groups were keen to assert how unpopular this was. For some, giving subordinates the credit for their work, encouraging those more capable than you to progress and shielding your team from the whimsy of higher management seemed like the obvious actions of a secure and competent manager. But for many, these superior strategies seemed like mistakes.

Often, the difficulty was that the skills that had allowed the managers to progress in management, such as personal ambition, aggressive self-promotion and independent problem-solving were ironically the skills that the paradigm had found made for less effective managers. This research turned out to be a hard sell because the focus group remained convinced that their skills were the most effective because they were successful managers, a conclusion that can be likened to a medieval doctor concluding that their leech remedies were the most effective because they were a successful doctor.

Despite this rocky start, the paradigm remained extremely popular amongst our sample groups. We initially assumed that the simplicity of the paradigm's central speed-aggression dichotomy was resonating strongly with their managerial styles but after further investigation it appeared that the paradigm was fulfilling a much more important role.

If things are going well, there are usually no shortage of explanations as to why, but when the situation darkens, when investors withdraw, negotiations stall or markets dry up, organizations are often left scrabbling for an easily understood explanation. The reality of a complex world filled with non-linear, interlocking variables far beyond the control of an entire industry let alone a single CEO or manager is often not just an unsatisfactory explanation but an uncomfortable glimpse of a disruptive truth.

It is a far greater comfort to imagine that your success is somehow the direct product of your efforts whilst your failures are the result of unforeseeable events, poor timing, restrictive legislation or just dumb luck. But of course, the converse could equally be true: your successes being the result of unforeseeable events, poor timing, restrictive legislation and dumb luck whilst your failures are the direct product of your efforts to do otherwise. That's not to say that all possible actions are equal or that your decisions have no impact, but rather that, any post hoc explanatory narrative you impose upon them is just that: a narrative.

And this is where the paradigm comes into its own. Rather than forcing an organization to develop a sense of perspective and to learn from their mistakes by delving into the complex reasons for failure, the paradigm offers simple exculpatory mechanisms such as: there wasn't enough speed. Or, there was too much aggression.

These easy-to-grasp excuses turned out to be particularly important for those managers who had shackled their ego to their economic success. Following this insight, we fully optimized the paradigm to cater for those who wish to engage in self-delusion.

INCREASING PROFITS

Businesses are always looking to report record profits and this is an admirable goal, however, as any experienced practitioner will tell you, there are sustainable methods of achieving record-breaking profits, such as employing the RN Paradigm, and unsustainable methods, such as employing the Levington process.

The RN Paradigm, when correctly applied, facilitates businesses in posting record profits, but the paradigm also shows us that perpetually increasing profits requires exponential growth. Your goal might be to achieve sustained exponential growth, but the RN Paradigm suggests that over extended timescales such growth is likely to consume more energy than is contained within the observable universe and thus might not be a realistic or desirable aspiration for a business.

Obviously, Levington accommodates record profits over the short term through wage reduction/stagnation and the liquidation of assets, a style of shareholder economics for which the RN Paradigm is not conventionally optimized. The paradigm is structured assuming that a business wishes to avoid short term annihilation in the pursuit of personal profit. However, a parallel extension of the model by Nillesen has resulted in the Nillesen polyphasic adjunct (NPA) a set of parameters which adequately describes the Levington process to a five-sigma significance. The NPA extension is not recommended for most businesses because of the dystopian world of extreme inequality it would usher in, but the adjunct is available for those businesses that are willing to pay our platinum-plus premium rate.

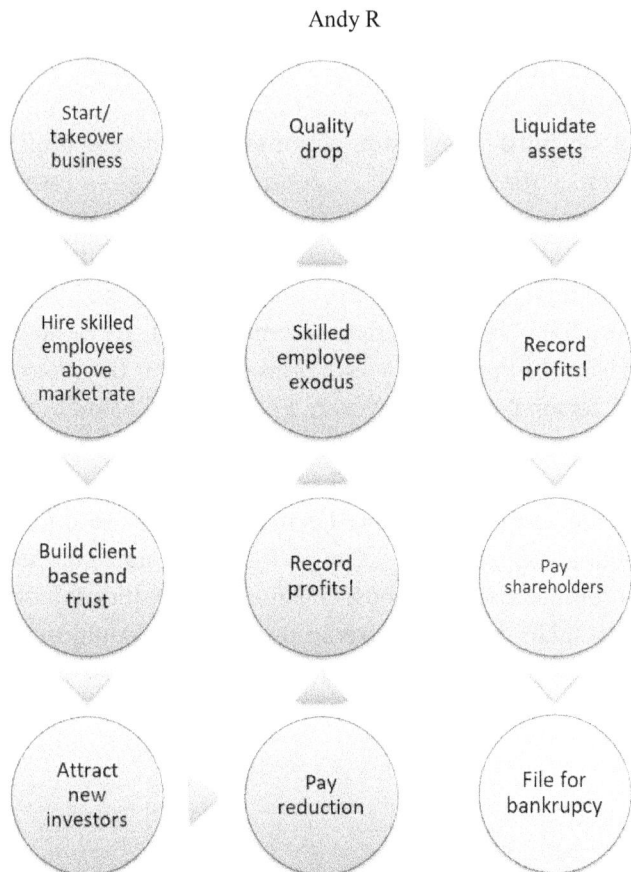

The Levington process (1982) as summarized in the 1985 book *Free Money: How to Win at Business*

INFORMATION

Through modelling a broad variety of businesses, the RN Paradigm concludes that the more information an organization has about their competitors the better able they are to make informed decisions. Informed decisions are consistently shown to outperform those decisions underpinned by whimsy and hearsay.

Get as much information as possible, even if it disagrees with your preconceptions.

Usually, organizations are encouraged to obtain as much information as possible and as Nillesen is quoted as saying, *"Get as much information as possible, even if it disagrees with your preconceptions."* Although, he later came to reject this idea once more information had come to light.

There is certainly an upper limit to the amount of information that is sensible for an organization to acquire. The RN Paradigm recommends that an organization avoids the Beckenstein bound, as exceeding this is likely to lead to collapse.

Most organizations control the flow of information through the medium of meetings and meetings are amongst the most effective mechanisms for decision-making. But meetings are also a gladiatorial arena in which the politics of power are played out. The savvy manager attends such meetings with the classic Leidenfrost axioms (1994) in mind:

Be bold: you might not understand what's being discussed, but that doesn't invalidate your random, uninformed suggestions.

Come unprepared: the point of the meeting is for everyone else to bring you up to speed.

Repetition: repeat the same point multiple times as the brilliance of your insight will eventually be recognized.

Stay relevant: assert confidently whatever pops into your head, otherwise people will forget you're in the room.

Focus on your strengths: when the meeting finally reaches something you know about, try and keep the meeting on that point for as long as possible.

Be a winner: meetings are usually won by whoever spoke the most and/or the loudest.

SPECIFIC CIRCUMSTANCES

In a shifting, external economy increased profits can usually be achieved by increasing your organization's velocity, making them faster and more responsive to the changes. The challenge for a business is in recognizing how the RN Paradigm applies to their specific set of circumstances and how to go about increasing their velocity accordingly. The difficulty is that a modern business is often composed of numerous divisions and it might be tempting to think that in order to increase your organization's velocity that every division must do so accordingly. However, an increase in velocity does *not* require all of a company's departments to increase their velocity and counter-intuitively may often require some departments to drop their velocity and increase their aggression. For example, a company wishing to increase its group velocity might have a legal department that needs to be more aggressive, a sales division that needs more velocity and a marketing division that needs to be operating with a balance.

Every market is different and every business is composed of different talents, thus the individual solutions are rarely the same. Whilst the path to success is manifold, the path to failure is well-trodden and it is worth picking up your copy of Eddington's inimical Codex of Common Business Mistakes and reacquainting yourself with the Data Analysis section of this timeless work.

Andy R

14a - Speculation is not information

- Regardless of how important someone is or how much experience they might have, their opinion does not supersede data on the situation and nor is it a substitute for actual data. Speculation can be useful, but it doesn't stop being speculation.

27r - A single data point is not a trend

- If the quarterly performance of a department dips, that single data point does not in itself constitute the start of a trend. Refrain from excessive intervention until you have sufficient information. It's also worth training your management in the concept of *regression to the mean*. Minor short-lived declines should elicit the same level of concern as minor short-lived increases.

31.7g - Over interpretation does not generate new information

- The behaviour of markets in the past is not a reliable indicator of how they will behave in the future. Excessive analysis of the past tells you about the past, excessive analysis of the future tells management that you need to be replaced.

82 - Random fluctuations occur

- Complex systems can exhibit random behaviour. Don't try to predict this, it's random. Don't try and conjure an explanation for these events, they're random. Ignore them and continue with what you were doing.

141a - Simple rules can produce complex behaviour

- A complex series of seemingly unrelated problems can sometimes have a single source, be it a bad manager or a difficult individual. However, more often than not...

141b - Single causes are rarely useful explanations

- If a self-proclaimed expert asserts that the recent market downturn is due to a single reason, such as the unions, oil prices, too many immigrants... etc. they're almost certainly wrong. In a complex system, a single cause is rarely to blame and subscribing to a single explanation cripples critical thinking and restricts your ability to respond.

Excerpts from the Data Analysis section of Eddington's *Codex of Common Business Mistakes*. First published 1973

BALANCE/HARMONY

Thus, we come to the conclusion that the RN Paradigm is not simply about aggression or speed. Crucially the RN Paradigm is about knowing when aggression is productive and when speed is necessary. If you are not aggressive in the marketplace you will be unable to compete. But equally too much aggression will increase resistance and begin to impinge upon your speed. If you don't have speed you will be unable to compete in the future, but too much speed and you run the risk of failing to adequately develop your markets. The RN Paradigm is about balancing these competing components and holding them in tension. Some analysts might choose to visualize the RN Paradigm as a literal balance, and this can be a useful introduction to the paradigm. Both speed and aggression are present at any one time, but on balance, the organization is either fast or aggressive depending on the number and weight of these components.

In this example, the business would appear to be aggressive, but at any moment the weight of these components could alter and the balance would necessarily shift. It is important to realize that there is no winner between speed and aggression; they are equal partners in driving the success of your business.

Of course, the full RN Paradigm is described through three elegant equations that parse speed and aggression as tensor fields permeating a market space and the actions of a particular business as perturbations within those fields as operated on by the specific business metric (SBM). The full solutions to these equations are extremely complex, but by carefully restricting certain degrees of freedom and utilizing some of the underlying symmetries, they can be simplified down to a series of colorful rectangles drawn on top of a triangle.

As explained earlier, the paradigm is particularly useful in post hoc application. After a contract negotiation collapses or a newly acquired business fails to even cover its capital costs, it is natural for organizations to seek an explanation. Unfortunately, a full explanation is often complex, multifaceted and difficult to summarize before a series of angry board members. However, by calling upon the radical simplicity of the RN Paradigm, an awkward explanation in terms of multiple factors can be safely collapsed into a simple call for either more speed or more aggression.

RICHMOND-NILLESEN PARADIGM TYPES

Pay a visit to the offices of any organization and it soon becomes apparent that there are a variety of different personalities. A successful manager is one who can utilize the different personalities within their organization and create teams with the right mixture of speed and aggression. The RN Paradigm is unique in the resolution with which it details twenty-eight easily identifiable types.

	Tanker		Ninja
	Hammer		Sniper
	Glory seeker		Grindstone
	Simplifier		Complainer
	Negotiator		Believer
	Manipulator		Amplifier
	Confident Guesser		Doubter
	Thinker		Career Traveler

HOW TO USE RN TYPES

At the top of each section, you will see a symbol and the name of the type. These will help you identify which RN type you are reading about.

 **Name of type**

How to identify:
> This section describes your key strengths and characteristics and describes the value that you bring to a team. This helps you identify this R/N type in either yourself or others.

How to manage:
> This section describes how best to manage this RN type and in what role they are best placed.

Speed: 0.0
> This assigns a speed value for this RN type.

Aggression: 0.0
> This assigns an aggression value for this RN type.

If you are using the RN basic package then these values will seem almost entirely meaningless. The RN premium package unlocks the true values which can be thought of as the speed-aggression manifold being projected onto a linear market-space.

Andy R

Tanker

By definition a Tanker is slow, but what the Tanker lacks in speed it more than makes up for with its phenomenal momentum, crushing the opposition and driving the organization forward.

How to identify:

Your primary values are ***action*** and ***confidence***. As a Tanker, you are full of information and experience and this makes you an invaluable employee. In the same way that Tankers are the unsung backbone of global trade, you are the backbone of any organization. You have a strong work ethic and, like the Grindstone, will steadily plough your way through the work and get things done. However, you are not dragged into details like the Grindstone. You are aware of the final objective and keep your eyes fixed on that horizon. Others can always rely on your level-headed, no-nonsense approach and in times of crisis you are the one that people will turn to for your steady wisdom and advice. Your wealth of experience has given you a confidence that others lack and in discussions and negotiations you have a clear sense of what needs to be done. You may find that others overcomplicate situations but you have the ability to see through this complexity and can power through the hot air and posturing to reach a conclusion that had been obvious to you from the start.

How to manage:

In the hands of a skillful manager, Tankers are invaluable. They can also be a massive liability. The Tanker carries on regardless of new information, which they will discount, and new objectives, which they will ignore. Tankers plough on with a project, obliterating objections through the sheer force of their conviction and ignorance. Tankers are almost completely impervious to counter arguments and so can be particularly useful in negotiations when your opponents are making some inconveniently valid points. Unfortunately, this recalcitrance to new information equally applies to your own arguments and so at the start of a project it is important to make sure you know in what direction your Tankers are pointing because once they get going, that's it. Inevitably society and your organization will move on but your old Tankers will be unable to adapt and unless you manage them carefully they will run aground and require a substantial clean-up operation. Before this situation occurs, consider promoting your old Tankers sideways into positions with great sounding titles but absolutely no impact on daily operations.

Specd: -8.0
Aggression: 11.2

Andy R

Hammer

Hammers are great for getting things done. They break things up, they knock teams into shape and they drive projects home. To a hammer, everything is a nail.

How to identify:

Your primary values are *action* and *resilience*. You like to get things done. In your view, the true objective of any project is its completion and the quicker and more efficiently a project can be completed the better. Like tearing off a Band-Aid, the swift solution is often the best solution and for you, this is equally true in business. You favor a one-touch approach to work, dealing with emails and events as they arise and where possible solving them on the spot. There are few things more satisfying than having colleagues come to you with a seemingly insurmountable problem only to pulverize that problem into a workable solution and hand it back to them completed. You have extremely high standards for your own work and expect others to have the same. You find weakness irritating and refuse to accept excuses for substandard work; if someone finds the work too difficult then they should be doing another job.

How to manage:

Hammers make some of the best middle-managers and deputies because they will carry out your instructions and make sure that everyone else will too. However, if your Hammer is given bad information or free rein over a project with minimal oversight, they can make a proper mess. Whilst having a Hammer oversee a division can seem like a surefire way of ensuring efficient and dynamic solutions, their inflexibility in accommodating different ways of working and insistence that everyone adopts the Hammer approach can lead to dissatisfaction and a loss of diversity. Eventually, you'll end up with an entire division of Hammers and a division of Hammers can break things apart very quickly. Make sure your Hammers are kept well informed.

Speed: 7.8
Aggression: 10.2

Hammers are capable of both speed and aggression but too many of them on your team and you may regret the speed and aggression of multiple Hammers acting in different directions.

Andy R

Confident Guesser

When a situation is particularly complex and nobody is certain of the outcome then a Confident Guesser has no problems making a decision.

How to identify:

Your primary value is *confidence*. You're not being arrogant, but it's probably fair to say that you're the single most useful person in the organization. You have a natural grasp of how things work and you can see the solution to problems that baffle the so-called experts. They often spend far too much time worrying about the details, but in the world of business it is sometimes irrelevant what the actual decision is, all that really matters is that somebody has the confidence to make that decision. You view meetings as an opportunity for others to present their ideas so you can select which one is the best and then confidently assert its merits. Your incredible intellect allows you to recognize when the details matter and when they don't, which is something that very few other people seem to have. You're nobody's fool.

How to manage:

As Charles Darwin observed "Ignorance more frequently begets confidence than does knowledge." Confident Guessers are as clueless as everybody else but they sound and look confident. They assert complete rubbish with total conviction and this *can*, in some limited situations, keep teams motivated and focused on an outcome. The Confident Guesser is completely oblivious to their own incompetence because the skills needed to assess their competence are the same skills needed to be competent. This makes them a complete liability in any field that has measurable outcomes or technical requirements and so it is best to use your Confident Guessers in marketing positions. At first glance, the Confident Guesser might appear similar to the Tanker, but where Tankers are pathologically averse to changing direction, Confident Guessers have the useless ability to confidently change their mind the moment new information appears, irrespective of whether they've understood that information. It is unwise to place Confident Guessers into any management position as they will confidently make decisions with all the consideration of a random number generator. However, many Confident Guessers wind up in management having been mistaken for Hammers.

Speed: 6.8
Aggression: 7.2

The Confident Guesser highlights the need to include the full Riemannian context when applying the RN Paradigm. Just because a role scores highly on both speed and aggression that does not mean that their role is intrinsically more important or that their decisions are beneficial, just that the role they perform, scores highly in both parts of the metric.

Andy R

 Ninja

Ninjas are, swift, silent and highly effective. They are masters of speed and provide permanent solutions to problems without needing to hang around and claim the credit.

How to identify:

Your primary values are ***humility*** and ***tranquility***. You enjoy your job and the position you have attained. You work hard, but never to the detriment of your health and your personal life. Like the passing of the seasons, you leave work on time. You cultivate relationships that nourish and fulfil and harvest information for the good of all. You are the soft silence before dawn. You see the solutions that are invisible to others and yet have the wisdom to know when those solutions should not be pursued. You are the peripheral glimpse of a receding shadow. You can navigate the interconnectedness of multiple operations with the agility of a swift on a summer's evening. You are not motivated by recognition or the decorative baubles of external validation. You prefer to instigate solutions with the lightest of touches, a suggestion here and a supposedly chance meeting there. If you happen to be in a position of power you will use your influence to effect seemingly minor adjustments that will be crucial for success but will go unnoticed by almost everyone. A lot can be achieved when it doesn't matter who takes the credit.

How to manage:

You can't manage a Ninja. If one day a seemingly intractable client suddenly become far more cooperative or indeed is replaced by someone else entirely, you may have a Ninja on your team. If you fire a quiet employee who never seemed to have the drive and ambition to really make it in this business and soon after projects and teams start to fall apart, you probably just fired a Ninja. Ninjas don't make themselves known other than through the solutions they leave behind.

Speed: 0.0
Aggression 0.0

You cannot know whether you have a Ninja on your team, you can only suspect. For this reason, you cannot add the effects of a Ninja into your Speed/Aggression metric calculations. If you 'know' that someone is operating like a Ninja then they're not a Ninja, they're either a Sniper or a Fixer, or you're a Confident Guesser.

Sniper

Snipers will take up a position outside the immediate combat zone and fire off accurate, highly effective solutions to problems. A sniper is proactive rather than reactive: they head problems off long before anyone else is aware that there was even a problem there. Snipers are by definition fast. They can adapt to new situations and have an informed overview of not just their situation, but everyone else's as well.

How to identify:

Your primary values are *knowledge* and *efficacy*. If you are a Sniper then the chances are you are both well-read and well-informed and have a sound understanding of most of the projects within the organization. Like the Ninja, you can see the solutions to problems that others will miss, but unlike the Ninja, you will either charge a consultancy fee for the solution or trade the information for improved standing. You are highly effective on the phone, in person and through email and you will seek to spot and eliminate problems before others are even aware that they could have been a threat.

How to manage:

Most Snipers come into the organization as troubleshooters or consultants, but if you're lucky enough to already have a Sniper in your outfit then it is a good idea to move them into a position that gives them access to a wide range of projects. Snipers can deliver solutions into projects that you may have written off as a lost cause and they can identify problems long before others in the group. In the hands of a Sniper a potentially difficult client can be made to seem straightforward and compliant, and a complex operation simple and self-sustaining, but do not underestimate the intelligence that has gone into making these happen. Far too many managers have lost patience with their Snipers and their apparent lack of results, failing to appreciate the subtle, long-range work that they undertake and thus replacing them with a more immediate Hammer or Simplifier. Of course, the consequences of replacing the Sniper won't be felt for some time because the Sniper works at such range, but eventually, the once simple project will become a complex disaster full or intractable problems and the once compliant client will become an unreasonable jerk. Most managers will fail to see that the problem was losing the Sniper six months earlier.

Speed: 12.7
Aggression: -1.3

Snipers will gradually accelerate a group or organization by reducing the external drag forces rather than through a reduction of the internal mass – as with the Simplifier. By reducing the drag the Sniper is able to accelerate a group up to velocities that would be completely unsustainable through the use of a Simplifier. Whilst using a Simplifier will accelerate the group rapidly, the accompanying turbulence eventually shakes the group apart. Turbulence ceases to be a problem for groups with a Sniper because the drag forces have been removed. This allows for sustained high velocities.

Andy R

Glory Seeker

Glory Seekers will often work on several projects for extended periods with seemingly no impact but once one of the projects breaks through and becomes successful it will transpire that they were instrumental to that success.

How to identify:

Your key skills are *networking* and *confidence*. You have realized that success is about knowing the right people and being in the right place at the right time. Rome wasn't built in a day and no man is an island. Teamwork is vital to the success of any project and you are an expert in getting teams to run smoothly but you worry that those above you don't understand the vital role that you play. Sometimes a team needs to be left to figure out the problems by itself, but when results start to happen, that's when you step in to help guide the team and steer them towards success. You are vital to the group and as one of those rare individuals with the confidence to make an honest appraisal of your abilities without being affected by false humility and the anxiety that you might appear arrogant, you are happy to celebrate your wins. Those who downplay their achievements are not doing themselves any favors.

How to manage:

When a project becomes successful it is natural to think about replicating that success with other projects. Reassigning key players is a great way of sharing good practice and raising the expertise of everyone in the organization. However, just because someone appears to be a key player that doesn't mean that they are. Glory Seekers will often claim credit for the work of others whilst being a dead weight themselves and they can be difficult to distinguish from truly competent team members. One method is getting someone to ask the team members who did most of the work; they usually know. As a manager, there's nothing wrong with having a few Glory Seekers on the team, they provide a level of self-promoting aggression and they have a surprising amount of insight into how well different projects are doing. But having too many on your staff reduces your power to weight ratio and makes your team sluggish and unable to respond to change.

Speed: 2.2
Aggression: 5.4

For each additional Glory Seeker: S_Q x 0.693, A_Q x 0.693

If you have more than one Glory Seeker on your team then each additional Glory Seeker reduces your team's overall speed and aggression by a factor of ln2 (0.69314)

Andy R

Thinker

Things are not always as they appear and what at first may look like a sharp investment might turn out to be a terrible business proposition. A Thinker is someone who takes the time to acquire and review data before making a decision. They are often suspicious of impulsive actions.

How to identify:

Your key values are *knowledge* and *patience.* You think of yourself as a rational, scientific person. For you, business is a complex system of competing interactions that can ultimately be understood through patient observation and the accumulation of data. Rather than making mistakes firsthand, you would rather see if others have faced similar decisions in the past and investigate their choices and their outcomes. You distrust simplification and view those who espouse it as foolish. The world remains complex no matter how much detail you choose to ignore or how much nuance you collapse into pithy observations. Pretending something is simple does nothing to diminish the complexity authoring your demise. For you, the solution is often about acquiring the most up-to-date information and then wading in and wrestling with the complexity until you've dragged out some useful information that you can piece together into a model.

How to manage:

A Thinker is one of the most aggressive components in your team. It might seem strange to consider a Thinker as engendering aggression, but thinking is a slow and deliberate act and once you have witnessed a true Thinker engaged in a negotiation you will understand just how overwhelmingly powerful cold hard facts can be. In the right hands, facts can crush opponents into submission and obliterate competitors with their glacial-like inevitability. However, despite their rationality and overall intelligence, it is often inadvisable to have a Thinker as a manager. Thinkers adhere to the facts no matter what, and this can make them a terrible motivator when the facts are really depressing. Thinkers are often slow at responding to rapid change as they will wait to assess the validity of the change before committing to it. This rigidity means that Thinkers make very few costly mistakes, but equally a Thinker will not operate anywhere near the cutting edge, preferring instead to work with well-understood technologies and employing well-established techniques. A prominent Thinker will greatly increase your team's mass and aggression but effectively rob them of their velocity as they question and derail any and all who would seek to accelerate the team.

Speed: -6.2
Aggression: 9.2

Andy R

Doubter

A Doubter occurs when a Thinker encounters data that conflicts with the views of management.

How to identify:
Your primary values are *knowledge* and *truth*. With every project you look long and hard at what is being asked. You source and scrutinize all of the available data but in this case, you have reluctantly come to the conclusion that management's decisions are misguided. You are a Doubter. Your stance is not personal; it is simply a product of the information. You appreciate that management's views might have been misinformed by a lack of up-to-date information, or may have resulted from a misunderstanding of what the data represents but you're convinced that as it stands, the project will fail. Everybody else in the team seems to be forging ahead, flinging themselves into their work like unthinking drones, fulfilling the absurd request of their masters, but you are standing back and looking at the bigger picture and seeing the problems that will arise if things continue as they are. To doubt is a bold and courageous response and whilst many teams may have Thinkers, very few teams have a Thinker strong enough and confident enough to turn against the tide of management and make a stand.

How to manage:

Doubters rarely understand the bigger picture that you are dealing with and will often come to you with irrelevant concerns that they think are overwhelmingly important, sometimes with data, but rarely with any workable solutions. Doubters corrode the unity and vision of the group and it is important to deal with them quickly. Most Doubters are just team members who want to complain about some minor aspect of their working conditions and these Doubters can be dealt with quickly by just hearing them out, a simple process of nodding occasionally and telling them you'll pass on their concerns, or by suggesting they find a less challenging job. Remember Doubters are a sign that you are not doing your job correctly so they need to be managed swiftly before your superiors learn of your shortfalls, or, if you're the director of the company before the shareholders learn of the insurrection.

Speed: -6.1
Aggression: -7.2

Andy R

Grindstone

The Grindstone is often the first employee to arrive and the last to leave. For the Grindstone the solution to a problem is to double down on their previous efforts and to work twice as hard as before. A Grindstone doesn't work smarter, a Grindstone works harder.

How to identify:
Your primary values are ***hard work*** and the satisfaction gained from a ***job well done***. Whilst others may cut corners and rush to get a job finished you know that if a job isn't done well, then it's not worth doing at all. You are proof that hard work solves problems and you become frustrated when colleagues quit before they have fully completed their work. You enjoy being lost in the tension and adrenaline of a deadline and whilst you will outwardly complain to others about the amount of work you have to do at home, a part of you secretly enjoys the structure and predictability it provides. You respect and understand those who work similar hours to you but you struggle to understand those who appear to do very little and yet remain not only employed but somehow praised.

How to manage:
Keep them working, but do so carefully. Many Grindstones use work as a way to mitigate their anxieties and suppress the demons that haunt their

private life, be it the whine of an unhappy marriage or just the yawning abyss of mortality that opens up whenever they experience free time. Grindstones are thus susceptible to burnout through a lack of self-regulation. Many Grindstones will complain about the amount of work they have to do and can be assuredly vocal over how it's destroying their life, but they will do nothing to alleviate the situation and will instead choose to lose themselves in their work once again. Thus many Grindstones either burnout or slam sideways into a midlife crisis.

Making a Grindstone into a manager might seem like a great idea because they can be so productive and so committed to the organization, but seriously, Grindstones make atrocious managers. Their main problem is a complete lack of trust in others: they don't really believe that anyone else can do the job quite as well as they can. Grindstones will micromanage everything, essentially slipping back into their old role – the one with which they are most familiar – and end up doing the work of their subordinates either to 'show' them how it's done or to 'get it done quickly'. They will sometimes post hoc rationalize this behavior as 'leading by example', but such actions are beneficial to no-one. It simultaneously undermines their authority as a manager and undermines the confidence of their subordinates. Grindstones often compensate for a lack of skill or understanding by quadrupling their efforts, a response that often robs them of the time and perspective that would have enabled them to address the underlying problem. Thus Grindstones can be oddly slow to adapt and learn, despite their insatiable commitment to do so. Whilst some Grindstones can eventually learn to become good managers, they do so by learning to stop being a Grindstone.

Speed: 0.752
Aggression: 6.82

The RN Paradigm

 # Simplifier

Complicated facts can slow projects down and that's where every project needs a Simplifier, someone who will compress the troublesome nuance and complexity out of a situation. When negotiations stall because clients need clarification over technicalities the Simplifier can step in and swiftly label their concerns as "being difficult" and thus free everyone up to move on.

How to identify:
Your values are *simplicity* and *brevity*. It is easy to complicate a situation, to wrap an idea in words and cover it with the thorns of multiple viewpoints but it takes someone with insight and wisdom to simplify a situation down to its essence. This is why we prize aphorisms and short quotes so highly. The progenitors of these quotes have managed to reach into a bulky, cumbersome idea and pare them down to a simple phrase that resonates with us all. You distrust those who use lots of information and data because in doing so they're obscuring the simple truths that people can readily grasp. You have the clarity of thought and vision to cut through the nonsense that others refer to as nuance and you have the social confidence to describe things the way they are. You find that if an idea takes more than a few seconds to explain then it's either not been explained well enough or it's not worth knowing. You don't doubt the existence of

complex ideas, but you understand that the more complex the idea the less relevance it has to the world in which we all live. You can summarize whole conferences in a few sentences and compress multiple weeks of negotiation into a few words. You can see where projects have gone wrong and have the perspicacity to assign blame.

How to manage:

Simplifiers are the epitome of acceleration. If you have a working group overburdened by information and indecision then the introduction of a Simplifier will reduce the group's mass and significantly alter their trajectory. The only thing that speeds up a project more than injecting a Simplifier into the mix is injecting two Simplifiers into the mix. Two Simplifiers will produce a mutual feedback loop that effectively destroys all extraneous information and produces the simplest world view possible. Some managers like to make their Simplifier a link person. A Simplifier's report will always be short and to the point and they will usually tell you that the project is going well. If things aren't going well then the Simplifier will provide you with a blunt run-down of who is to blame and the team-leaders can go from there. If you work in a business that produces nothing of any real significance or utility, you can apply as many Simplifiers as you like.

Simplifiers can be superficially similar to Confident Guessers, however, Simplifiers are not necessarily ignorant, they just don't like or trust complexity.

It is advisable to keep Simplifiers away from engineers, scientists, medical professionals, legal departments and industries situated in the real world.

Speed: 10.75
Aggression: -7.2

+50% speed bonus for being teamed with another Simplifier.

Complainer

The Complainer is always the victim. They would rather have the excuse than the success.

How to identify:
Your core strength is a sense of **dissatisfaction** with the world. You think the world could be much better than it currently is and you're prepared to wait until someone gets round to sorting that out.

How to manage:
It's important to realize that just because someone is complaining, that does not mean they are a Complainer. There may be legitimate reasons for complaints and a good manager will address those without prejudice.

The true Complainer will rarely elevate their complaints to a formal level, but will instead make themselves known to colleagues by complaining about pretty much everything: the weather, the coffee, the news, their kids, other people's kids, cars, walking, existing, computers, TV, Wi-Fi, work, holidays.

The tragedy of the Complainer is that often they really don't want to be in their job. That's not to say they don't deserve the job, or are unsuited to the job, or are incompetent. It's that they lack the self-belief to appreciate their own abilities and thus they lack the self-confidence to find a job that they would otherwise enjoy. Trapped by their own insecurity or even the familiarity of abdicating responsibility, they often become the author of their own misery.

Many Complainers either get fired, giving them yet another thing to complain about and confirming their sense of being a victim, or undergo some personal growth through support and counselling and thus transition into another category.

Unsurprisingly, their unrelenting negativity impacts both speed and aggression. This can be useful.

Speed: -7.0
Aggression -7.0

 # Career Traveler

The Traveler has journeyed from a distant organization or position where their actions are thought to have made a significant difference. They are often hired to shake things up in an attempt to bring some of the magic that worked so well at their last position.

How to identify:

As a Traveler your core beliefs are ***action*** and ***idealism***. In your last position, you took a sub-optimal workforce that thought they knew best and through your system and your aggressive management you set in motion a transformation that is probably still continuing today. You like coming into an organization and seeing the structures and assumptions with fresh eyes. You are unbound by any history and immune to the refrain 'it's always been done like this,' and your clear perspective allows you to make the sweeping changes that others need. You work hard and feel everyone should do the same. You achieve high levels of productivity by focusing on individual monitoring and when standards fall short of your expectations you hold people accountable. Your systems have an immediate impact and your superiors are invariably impressed. Your legendary improvements in productivity allow you to move on to pastures new and to carry on up the career ladder. You often have to leave the details of completion for others.

How to manage:

The Career Traveler likes to slam into an organization and upset all those stuck in their ways. Ironically, the Career Traveler sticks to what they know: paying scant attention to the specifics of the new organization and instead of hitting hard with the same system that worked last time. There are people who can instigate lasting and productive changes, usually Snipers and Thinkers, who will stay with their organizations for several years but these productive changes are almost never made by the Career Traveler. The Career Traveler attempts to change large amounts quickly and with little to no sensitivity. The temporary rise in productivity is often the sort of temporary rise that accompanies almost any novel change to the working environment, an effect psychologists refer to as the *Hawthorne Effect* or the *Demand Effect*. The increased productivity is invariably unsustainable and the demands made of the workers often causes key individuals to burnout or to resign in protest. Of course, these detrimental effects take more than a few years to emerge but by that time the Career Traveler has already moved on to peddle their brilliance elsewhere. Career Travelers are rarely malevolent and often believe their own hype. They're a little like the driver who only ever seems to see car accidents in their rearview mirror. They happily misinterpret the wreckage their systems have triggered as showing what happens when their leadership is removed. Before hiring this season's transformational wunderkind, make sure they've worked in their previous post for several years.

Speed: **8.0** initially and **-4.2** for each additional year.
Aggression:2.0 then **-1.2** for each year.

Classifier

Classifiers are members of the team who take unique and idiosyncratic problems and categorize them as belonging to sets of previously encountered problems. The Classifier will give these sets of problems catchy names so that the team can easily recall and relate to them and this can help the team speed up their problem solving.

How to identify:

Your key values are *simplicity* and *knowledge*. When you look at the world you see connections and patterns that make seemingly isolated and complex phenomena far easier to grasp and to understand. Confronted with a bewildering range of flora and fauna botanists and zoologists have systematically named animals and placed them into groups and subgroups that help explain their connections to each other. You similarly see the business world as a zoo within which we can classify people, systems and problems and then use those classifications to help us in the future. Most situations will have been encountered at some point before but most likely they will have been forgotten about. By classifying things and giving them memorable names a business can more readily identify those problems when they arise and take shortcuts to solutions that have already been obtained elsewhere.

How to manage:

At first glance, a Classifier can look a lot like a Simplifier, and in some ways they are. However, the Classifier is driven by the illusion of control that labelling things can deliver, whereas the Simplifier belittles complexity from an unspoken anxiety that they might not be smart enough.

Having a Classifier might seem like a great idea for an organization and to a certain extent, it can speed up certain decision-making processes and provide adequate solutions to restricted problems sets. Many Classifiers end up offering their insights and beliefs to organizations for a fee and with the Classifier's elaborate explanatory mechanisms and pseudo-scientific jargon many organizations will feel they are getting something substantial in return. However, there is a danger for organizations to succumb to the nomothetic fallacy. In this, groups can delude themselves into thinking that they have either gained an understanding or solved a problem simply because they've found a name for it. And Classifiers, by sticking labels onto events or people in a complex world, can give the impression that they have accessed a profound and underlying structure to that world whereas in reality all they have done is stuck a noun on a thing. As a manager, you must decide whether your Classifier is helping or hindering.

Speed: 8.1
Aggression: 3.5

The RN Paradigm

Believer

Believers are always bang up-to-date with the most recent and most effective management techniques and they truly believe that they work.

How to identify:

Your key values are ***communication*** and ***belief***. There are a lot of different techniques and ways of implementing management strategies. Some focus on the large scale picture, the meta-narrative of management, and some look at the detail, the nitty-gritty of what makes up a good team and how people get along with each other. You have read many of these techniques, but they have always just seemed dry and disconnected from the reality that you and your colleagues inhabit. But recently you have started reading this one book that has turned out to be a complete revelation. It's unlike anything else you've read. It's not just that this book makes really great rational arguments based on facts and figures and provides nice simple analogies and readily accessible anecdotes, it's more than that. You've been struck by just how *true* it feels. As you've been reading you've been making connections with your own life and your own experiences. This book has triggered so many inspirational ideas that you've been left with an unquenchable desire to help others obtain this same sense of enlightenment and you really believe that this system could benefit your organization.

How to manage:

Believers are usually new to the organization and extremely idealistic. If they've got a good system, they'll revitalize your organization, if not, they'll crash and burn. Believers are usually a positive influence on the team, enhancing their speed or aggression depending on what the group needs unless they've adopted a contradictory system, in which case they'll have the opposite effect.

Speed/Aggression: +7.0 (if it's the right system - 8.2 if it's the wrong one)

If your Believer is consistently changing the management system, they're a special brand of Believer: the **Serial Believer**. Serial Believers should be distrusted. Anyone that can passionately argue for one system one week and then ditch it the next, is far too unpredictable and unstable to have in a cohesive team.

Serial Believer: Speed: -9.0
Aggression: -9.0

The RN Paradigm

Dissenter

The Dissenter instinctively adopts an oppositional position regardless of its merits.

How to identify:
Your key assets are *perception* and *individuality*. Those around you seem oblivious to the game that management is playing. You do your job and you do it well but you take umbrage at the nonsensical goals and expectations that management places upon you. Their endless cavalcade of management strategies and monthly targets are little more than anxious hand-wringing. The panic-stricken desire for control and their clamorous interventions are nothing more than the frantic self-assurances of an ego wanting to believe it's making a difference. You freely admit that some of the measures that management brings in are entirely reasonable, but their sheer number detracts from your primary goal of efficiently undertaking your job. You are generally distrusting of management but you reserve a special brand of contempt for those who employ buzzwords without an accompanying sense of irony.

How to manage:
The Dissenter might seem like a Doubter, but a Doubter has reached their position in deference to the evidence whereas a Dissenter holds their belief in spite of the evidence. The Dissenter will instinctively take

an oppositional position and scoff derisively at both the status quo and at any attempts to change it, regardless of their merits. It is for this reason that you must lay aside your ego and accept that the Dissenter hates what you're doing, whatever it is. Do not try to win over the Dissenter by appealing to their emotions and certainly avoid trying to employ evidence for this is a foolish endeavor. Evidence may convince the Doubter, but the Dissenter has not reasoned themselves into their reproach. Whatever your well-reasoned justifications may be, to the Dissenter they will sound pompous and fatuous. Many managers will thus try to eliminate Dissenters in the belief that they will undermine and erode their authority but this too can be a mistake, for in the right hands the Dissenter can be made into an extremely useful tool. Dissenters are usually of higher than average intelligence and, like the Thinker, are frequently eloquent individuals. This eloquence coupled with their innate rejection of authority can make them superb troubleshooters of struggling projects, where they will zero in on the flaws, as well as frustrating and slowing down difficult negotiations. Effectively managing a Dissenter is mostly about giving them projects that appeal to their intellect and capacity for problem-solving and then completely ignoring them when they complain before, during and after the transition.

Speed: -4.0
Aggression: 6.8 (but when strategically located, can be as high as 8.4)

The RN Paradigm

 # Negotiator

If there's a contract where the details need working through, then the meticulous questioning of a Negotiator is invaluable. If there's a price to be settled with a supplier, then the smooth talking Negotiator is the star. When colleagues or contractors disagree and lines of communication become compromised, then a Negotiator's ability to see multiple perspectives and to speak wisdom into people's lives allows them to bring everyone back to the table and to broker mutually beneficial compromises.

How to identify:

Your core strengths are ***communication*** and ***understanding***. You take the time to listen to individuals and their concerns because you have recognized that when a team works together it can achieve far more than when it is pulling in different directions. You seek a productive harmony in which your team communicates effectively between themselves and with others. When it comes to meeting complex needs there can be no one-size-fits-all, a productive relationship with a contractor or a client can only come from an understanding of their specific needs and that understanding can only come from listening. Many businesses like to make sweeping generalizations and will often reject 'compromise' as being a dirty word, but you understand that a compromise is an inherently positive idea. A compromise requires both sides to invest their time or resources, but ultimately both are receiving more from the agreement than they would without. You take the time to understand a situation before asserting your views, but when you do, you are able to do so forcefully and convincingly.

How to manage:

Negotiators are absolutely great if you have something that needs negotiating or if new members are struggling to integrate into the team. However, in situations where speed is paramount then your Negotiator can end up generating drag as they will keep reminding you that details overlooked now are likely to become details that generate expensive litigation later. Equally in situations where aggression is paramount then a Negotiator's desire to produce harmony and a mutually profitable compromise can end up undermining your Ozymandias-like stance of crushing all before you and having warriors sing songs about your mythic conquests.

Speed: 5.7 (+1 if they're working with you, -3 against.)

Aggression: 4.2 (+3.3 for, -2.8 against)

 Demander

The Demander is the immovable rock against which multi-million dollar deals can become shipwrecked.

How to identify:

Your core values are *justice* and *tenacity*. You have a strong sense of what should and shouldn't be in the world and you will not allow yourself to be swayed from your goal by the noises of disagreement or discontent. You have the single-minded vision and purpose to drive your agenda forward. You know that your suggestions are so important that a project or a deal will ultimately fail without them and so you fight hard to ensure that others don't make the terrible mistake of ignoring your insights. You work extremely hard, far harder than other people do but your genius and vision often seem to go unrecognized or unnoticed. Fortunately, your tenacity gives you the ability to make your insights heard and give you the strength to ride out the ignorance of your opponents.

How to manage:

Demanders are a pain in the ass. They are similar to a Tanker in their single-mindedness and immunity to outside input, but where the Tanker acts on behalf of the organization, the Demander is entirely selfish. They are not concerned with whether or not the deal works; they simply want their clause or idea included.

If they don't get what they want, nobody gets anything. Once you identify a Demander it is vital that you keep them well away from any positions of power. A Demander is completely ignorant of their own incompetence and their suggestions, clauses and ideas are usually damaging nonsense but their recalcitrance in accepting new information means they are rarely able to understand this. At first glance, a Demander can be easily confused for a Hammer or a Tanker but the Demander's monomaniacal fixation on their own output usually distinguishes them from the more holistic Tanker and the more action-orientated Hammer. A Demander is thus a powerful tool of aggression but one that must be implemented with extreme care. The skills needed to manage a Demander are similar to the skills needed to manage a toddler or a petulant teenager: you either tell them what's going to happen and ignore the subsequent tantrums, or you allow the Demander to believe that they've come up with the idea or clause that you want integrating into the project. Once you have installed a Demander into a team do not try to move them anytime soon, they are slow to learn new systems and are quick to feel out of their depth. It is a good idea to have a Negotiator on the same team, not because the Negotiator will be able to change the Demander, but because the Negotiator will help the rest of the team cope with the Demander's irritating foibles.

Speed: -6.00
Aggression: 13.00

Fixer

The situation is spiraling out of control, the deadline is looming and a healthy sense of panic has gripped the team. Ideas and potential solutions are being thrown around like confetti but they are all flimsy suggestions with no weight and no hope of success. Enter, the Fixer.

How to identify:

Your key skills are ***pragmatism*** and ***problem-solving***. You have worked on a thousand different projects with a thousand different people; you have seen companies soar to dizzying heights on the wings of careful planning and then crash back to earth under the weight of competition; you have watched great ideas rise up from the foundations of informed discussion and then stood back and watched them burn to ash in the fires of bad management. Now when you encounter a failing project you don't just see the mistakes and familiar flaws that you've seen a hundred times before, but their solutions, the actions that will mitigate the damage and in some cases, solve them. You are not interested in gathering the acclaim of colleagues or in cultivating favor amongst management, your concern is with fixing the problem and salvaging the work of others. Your experience gives you the distance and the overview needed to dispassionately assess the best course of action.

How to manage:

When things are going well your Fixer can often seem like an uninspiring member of the team: they're not going to be conjuring up innovative schemes, wowing clients with their slick presentations or putting in the extra hours to impress you. No, the fixer enters the fray when things are going wrong. Unlike the proactive Sniper, who heads off the problem before anyone even knew that there might have been one, the Fixer is a reactive component who responds to the problems that have arrived on your doorstep. It doesn't matter what the origins of the problems are, be they a Career Traveler who has moved on, a Confident Guesser being wrong or maybe even a Demander going full doomsday; to the Fixer, all that matters is salvaging some kind of working solution. And 90% of the time they will mend it and they will make it work, but be aware that the Fixer will always do what is needed and not necessarily what is popular. To that end, if your ego is tied up in a failing project, maybe a project that you've started or overseen, then it is worth reviewing whether you really want the solutions that a Fixer can provide, because in their solutions the Fixer will be blind to your role and will not care whether they make you look bad.

A lot of people like to imagine that they're no-nonsense Fixers but usually, they're just Confident Guessers asserting their solutions with unwarranted conviction. It's worth noting there are virtually no young Fixers: Fixers are forged in battle and tempered with experience. The true Fixer wastes no time in seeking acclaim, but rather just gets on with fixing things. Once you've identified them and you've decided that you want things fixed, give them the space and resources to recover what they can and bear in mind that whatever they salvage is better than the alternative. Fixers have the unique ability to dynamically adjust their speed/aggression components in response to each situation.

Speed: 0.0 – 9.8
Aggression: 0.0 – 9.7

Andy R

Amplifier

Amplifiers tell you exactly what you want to hear.

How to identify:
You are either *fantastically naïve* or *massively cynical.* Either way, you sit in meetings and agree vociferously with those in power. Whatever it is they're suggesting, you are 100% behind it, either because you lack the critical faculties to adequately assess what they're saying, or because your boss has a desperate need for external validation and you're seeking promotion.

How to manage:
There probably aren't any Amplifiers on your staff at all. All the agreement and accolade that keeps coming your way is probably a product of your brilliant insights and vision.

Amplifiers enhance the speed or aggression of those they agree with, irrespective of whether that's useful or not. But, hey, there aren't any on your team, right.

Speed: +0.0 +4.0i (the imaginary component has the effect of rotating the speed metric)

Aggression: +1.0 3.4i -5.0j 6.2k (An Amplifier's aggression is a quaternion that doesn't transform with any other value and is thus unable to be represented)

The RN Paradigm

 # Imitator

An Imitator looks like a manager, talks like a manager, behaves like a manager and makes decisions that seem like the kind of decisions that a manager would make.

How to identify:
Your key skill is *acting like a manager*. Through your career, you've been lucky enough to work with some exceptional managers and each time you've watched how their decisions have driven progress and their vision has sparked change. You've attended conferences on how to successfully manage projects and sat through seminars on how to effectively manage people and at each you've made meticulous notes and taken onboard their teachings and wisdom. You've taken the time to read every major management guide from the last two decades and humbly consider yourself something of an expert in the terminology and the concepts they employ. You know how to hire and fire people, how to assign different roles and how to respond when people ask you questions. You are a manager because you manage people and things.

How to manage:
The Imitator acts like a manager but has little to no understanding of what underpins a good decision or an effective action and hopes that through mimicry of

another's actions they can replicate their results. An Imitator is often well-meaning but ultimately ignorant of the contextual basis behind the skills needed to effectively manage or make intelligent decisions. They are like a child dressed in a white lab coat and pressing a stethoscope to their friend's chest; they have absolutely no understanding of what the stethoscope does or what it might be telling them, but they know that it works for doctors and so imagine that it will work for them too. Most of the time an Imitator will function as a reasonable manager because when the situations are routine, the decisions will follow a familiar structure. However, in the event of a novel situation the Imitator, now operating without precedent, has nothing to mimic and so starts making decisions that are essentially plucked at random from their past experience. They will justify these with impressive phrases drawn from their management lexicon but these linguistic arrangements are merely deckchairs aboard the Titanic and will do nothing to stop the impending calamity.

Some may be tempted to avoid using an Imitator altogether because of what could go wrong, but this would be a mistake. A carefully positioned Imitator, correctly harnessed can be made into an extremely productive manager, so long as they are kept away from cutting-edge projects or any environment where unpredictability is expected.

Operating within familiar routine:
Speed: 1.5
Aggression: 2.2

In dealing with the new and unfamiliar, values can vary depending on the uniqueness of the situation, but they will usually vary around a median negative value.

Speed: -5.2 (+/- 6.0)
Aggression: -4.1 (+/- 6.1)

Andy R

Derailer/ Expendable asset

Occasionally management will assign a project to someone for whom it seems completely unsuited. For example, if a project to design computer software for financial institutions was assigned to someone completely ignorant of computing, coding, marketing and finance. There are two possibilities: the first is that management are complete idiots, the second is that they have assigned the project to an Expendable Asset/Derailer

How to identify:

You're not really sure what your key strengths are. Maybe, *trying really hard*? In the past you have been repeatedly overlooked for promotion; colleagues who have joined the organization after you, have managed to rise in both position and responsibility but you cannot see what they possess that you do not. You have asked for feedback on what you could do to improve and to get ahead but when they go through things, you can't really see what they're talking about. Now, however, you seem to have cracked it. You've been asked to head up a project all of your own. You are now on an equal footing with all those who got promoted before you and you even have your own office. You had a look at some of the paperwork the other night however, but you only really understood about 10% of it. The project seems quite complicated and people keep mentioning major difficulties, but you're not really sure what they are or how you would go about solving them. You're pretty sure you can sort them out though, or maybe find an expert who knows how to solve them.

How to manage:

There comes a point when a project outlives its useful life. Most of the time this transition can be easily managed, but there can be instances where simply pulling the plug on a project is not feasible. Sometimes the difficulty can be due to the people that are invested in the project, or it could be an instance where the project's failure will reflect badly upon senior managers and their team. In these situations, a Derailer may be the solution. The Derailer usually lacks critical-thinking skills and so is unlikely to question why they have suddenly acquired a mature project of considerable complexity and difficulty, any more than they will have understood why they were previously passed up for promotion. A Derailer will slow a project down to such extent that it will usually spiral into oblivion. In the resulting wreckage, fingers may well be pointed at your Expendable Asset, which is fine since they are, after all, expendable. If there is no backlash or any call for scapegoats then your Expendable Asset can simply be reassigned to another failing project, or placed on hold until they are required again.

Speed: -13.0
Aggression: 0.00

Andy R

Manipulator

The Manipulator is a cross between a Dissenter and a Negotiator. Much like the Dissenter, who sees the world as being populated with incompetence, the Manipulator sees the world as a hostile place populated by those seeking to screw them over.

How to identify:
Your key strengths are *perception* and *winning.* You know that the world is a hostile place full of people who will take advantage of you the moment you let down your guard. Of course, it would be easier if it wasn't this way, but it is what it is and wanting it to be something else doesn't change anything. If you want to succeed you don't sit around waiting for success to come to you, you have to go out and create the opportunities yourself; you have to seize the initiative before someone else beats you to it. The business world isn't about making people happy or trying to keep as many friends as possible, no, the business world is about winning and that usually means winning at the expense of someone else. You enjoy using expressions like: "If you can't stand the heat, get out of the kitchen", "It's a dog-eat-dog world" and "That's what they want you to believe."

How to manage:
The Manipulator constructs great walls of distrust to form an impenetrable fortress against which they

repel all as invaders. The Manipulator can initially seem like a great negotiator, with their sharp insight and aggressive positioning, they can battle their way through hostile negotiations like a jungle-warrior wielding a machete, which is fine if all your negotiations are hostile. However, The Manipulator habitually views everything as a trap and thus, like a jungle-warrior returning to civilian life, the Manipulator struggles to adapt to the more routine aspects of business, such as negotiations and relationships based on trust and mutual benefit. The Manipulator negotiates hard and assumes the worst in others regardless of whether it's appropriate and whilst this might sound like a strong, pragmatic position, it often turns out to be less than so. Distrust begets distrust and over time a Manipulator will erode a working relationship into a wary, mutual animosity. They lack the versatility of a true Negotiator, but this does not, however, render the Manipulator useless, far from it; the Manipulator can be a highly effective employee when placed in the correct environment. Like the Dissenter, The Manipulator is good at rallying people into outrage.

Speed: 3.5
Aggression: 8.4

Andy R

Victimizer

The Victimizer believes that the department is riddled with incompetence and they delight in stories and situations that support this view.

How to identify:

Your core strengths are *hard work* and a strong sense of *justice*. You feel that you work hard and that you are good at your job. You are. You really are. But, you know, sometimes you have private doubts: maybe you're not quite good enough? But then you look around you and it seems obvious that a lot of people are, quite frankly, not pulling their weight. You work long hours and they don't seem to; you like to keep meticulous notes and file things in colored binders and they don't; you dress smartly and they don't seem to. These are all indicative of their incompetence. You wouldn't ever say it to their faces though, that would be rude, but you're quite happy to talk about it at length behind their backs and with their colleagues until their general perception is aligned with your own.

How to manage:

If the Victimizer has no managerial power, they're little more than the office gossip, undermining their colleagues in the hope of appearing marginally better themselves. However, a good leader can harness their petty vindictive nature by suggesting they implement or operate a performance management system that quantizes people's output by assigning numerical values to completely arbitrary measures of performance. Victimizers adore judging others and the numerical component makes them feel justified in their petty victimizing of colleagues.

If a Victimizer happens to wind up in a managerial role, they will usually strut around like they own the place, passing judgements, belittling their subordinates (usually behind their backs) and revelling in all the privileged information that their position gives them. Since the Victimizer is only really suited to creating a pernicious atmosphere of distrust and dissatisfaction, they can be useful if your goal is to slow down a project or to downsize a department, otherwise, it's a good idea to jettison them. If you enjoy irony, one method of eliminating two Victimizers with one action is to team them up together; over time they will mutually annihilate, usually through stress and ill health. In case you missed the irony, this action makes you a Victimizer too.

Beneath the veneer of numbers, unfocussed aggression and the evaporating wisps of their professionalism, the Victimizer is really a pathetic figure, forever blighted by their own inadequacy and the knowledge that their fleeting success is predicated on the downfall and misery of others. However, before you indulge in that pity, you should first hear what they have to say about you.

Speed: -9.8
Aggression: -5.1

Andy R

 # Networker

The Networker walks up to you at the conference, introduces themselves and then spends a few minutes laughing a little bit too much at your jokes and maintaining a little bit too much eye contact. Ten minutes later they'll be laughing with someone else and casually mentioning your earlier conversation as though you were old friends, something they will reinforce by either abbreviating your name down to something you've never before encountered, like Big A, or giving you a spurious nickname, like Beast.

How to identify:

Your primary skills are *communicating* and *confidence*. You understand that business is not about what you know but who you know. To this end you maintain a large and complex web of relationships that allow you to bypass the usual channels of communication and make links that allow you to leverage an advantage in negotiations or gain an edge in procurement. You benefit the whole team by putting colleagues in contact with experts.

How to manage:

Whilst it is significantly advantageous for any employee to have the skills of a Networker, the true Networker has taken the mantra "it's not what you know, but who you know," to a whole new level. The true Networker will effectively unburden themselves from all practical knowledge and become a purely social entity, an ethereal coordinator, setting up meetings and linking those with useful skills and information whilst maintaining no engagement or understanding of the project themselves. There is absolutely nothing wrong with this style of management and, aside from Networkers coming across as disingenuous and maybe a bit socially forward, they can make effective managers. However, a Networker remains effective only so long as they remain aware of their own ignorance. A self-aware Networker will continue to bring in experts and defer decisions to those with understanding, but more often than not Networkers wind up drinking their own Kool-Aid and concluding that they're as capable of making decisions as these so-called experts and start overriding the wisdom of those with actual information. At this point, their project is doomed as your Networker has transitioned into Confident Guesser.

A Networker has no intrinsic speed or aggression of their own because they have no knowledge of their own. However, they greatly enhance the attributes of everyone on their team.

Speed: 0.0 (x2 all those in the group)
Aggression: 0.0 (x2 all those in the group)

If your Networker goes rogue and begins going it alone, they halve the group's speed and aggression each quarter.

Andy R

Dictator

For the Dictator, exercising power is an end in itself. Like anxious royalty, a Dictator will assign tasks simply to assert that they are in a position to assign that task.

How to identify:

Your key skills are **having power** and **exercising power**. You're the alpha dog, the pack-leader and you're where you are because you're the best at what you do. You've worked hard to achieve your current position and those around you need to remember that. A team works best with strong decisive leadership and the role of your staff is ultimately to act upon your wisdom. You think of yourself as a people person, but you cannot abide insubordination – which you think of as being any subordinate pointing out flaws in your actions or understanding.

How to manage:

At some point in a Dictator's life, they have made a connection between having authority and having self-worth. Thus, each time they bark an order and a subordinate scurries away, they receive a frisson of self-worth that momentarily warms their soul before evaporating like morning dew. Sadly, each time an order is barked or a subordinate reprimanded, that moment of warmth grows shorter and less intense. The great tragedy of these moments is in their failure to accumulate. A lifetime of barking orders leaves the Dictator as empty of validation at the end of their career as they were at the start.

Most Dictators rise to some level of management determined by the equilibrium between their incompetence and their ambition, but they will usually remain in that position for most of their working life. Most organizations will have their share of Dictators and they usually make terrible managers. Since the exercise of power is almost always their goal, they are terrible at taking advice offered by subordinates and will often get sidetracked in meetings and negotiations by the need to appear in control. Even if the Dictator has a good understanding of what's required, they will often succumb to requiring staff to demonstrate their loyalty through meaningless acts of subservience that ties up valuable time and resources. On the plus side, Dictators are irrationally impressed by the power of their superiors and this makes them relatively easy to manage. However, it also means that if you want projects to succeed you will have to take the lead and the Dictator is likely to take up a lot of your time seeking your validation in the process.

A department run by a Dictator is usually dominated by Amplifiers and purged of its critical thinkers.

Speed: 0.5
Aggression: 12.2

Andy R

Panicker

The Panicker overturns folders and knocks pens to the floor as they frantically rummage through the papers on their desk. They're a very busy person. So busy. So, very, very busy. They glance up at you with a hunted expression. It's here somewhere. Then they remember: they've already signed the birthday card and passed it onto Barry.

How to identify:

Your key skills are **hard work, being busy** and having a strong sense of **perspective**. You understand how important things are and find the laid-back attitude of others confusing and annoying. You've worked hard to get this project to where it is and yet no one else seems to understand. There's still so much to do and you're busy doing it; not like everyone else. They don't seem to be responding with an appropriate sense of urgency at all. It's all up to you; you're the last bulwark against total failure. You're very important.

How to manage:

Like many people, a Panicker is searching for meaning in life and like many others, they have ended up attempting to derive that meaning through their work. The Panicker loudly huffs and puffs in a performance designed to convey both the importance and the amount of work that they are doing, building up to a crescendo of frantic disarray where they hurtle from moment to moment with all the situational awareness of a deer in headlights.

Panickers can make reliable team members as they will work hard and take their tasks seriously. However, they tend to make poor managers as the need for everything to seem important drives a lack of perspective that renders them almost incapable of balanced assessment.

Speed: 3.2 unless they're in full panic, in which case −7.2.

Aggression: 2.3

Category 5
Chaos Engine

A Chaos Engine is less of an individual than they are a force of nature.

How to identify:

You are awesome. Your key skills are **everything**. Everyone loves you. You are the single most intelligent human being to have ever existed. You can do nothing wrong. You have the Midas touch.

Except that sometimes on a rainy Sunday afternoon, when you are sitting alone watching the water bead down the window, you wonder if these things that you constantly tell yourself and others, might not be completely true. If only you could show your parents how successful you had become? Surely that would end this ache. But your parents are gone and you are alone. All that is left is the power. People will love you if you have power. Yes. Everyone will love you.

How to manage:

What is wrong with you? You can't manage a Chaos Engine any more than you can ride a tornado. It is sheer hubris to imagine that you can utilize their output. A Chaos Engine is by definition unpredictable and their erratic decisions are almost unrelated to initial inputs. They are seemingly immune to new information – except when they suddenly aren't – and usually appear to have no clue what they are doing. They are shot through with crippling insecurities and yet act with irrational levels of confidence, which can seem like a very appealing trait if you discount literally everything else about them. The scope of their disruption and devastation is proportional to the power that they wield. The only sensible strategy is containment. Chaos Engines are rare and if suitably contained, pose little risk. The danger only really arises when some idiot imagines they can ride the tornado to further their own agenda. As has already been stated, you can't and it won't.

Aggression: There is no meaningful value that can be written here.

Speed: Seriously, if you think you can assign a value to this, you haven't understood what chaos is.

Andy R

Individual

An Individual is someone who doesn't fit into any of the RN categories and so belongs in a category of their own. The Individual can have a dizzying variety of skills and personality traits that must be assessed by the manager on a case by case basis. Once you have assessed their strengths and weaknesses it's a good idea to place the Individual in a team with people who complement their skills and with whom they work well. This will help them and the other team members foster a productive working relationship.

Each Individual has different levels of speed and aggression.

COMMON QUESTIONS ABOUT THE PARADIGM

I and my colleagues have found that visionaries who introduce this book to their peers, colleagues, bosses, children or passing strangers, often get asked the same sort of questions. How well they answer these questions can often make the difference between a staggering success and horrific failure.

Here are some of those questions along with their answers that we have found to be helpful.

But we already have a way of thinking about thinking: why do we need a new way of thinking?

It's quite possible that you don't need to change the way you think. The RN Paradigm is only designed to be used by those who wish to be successful; there's no requirement for anybody to try anything they don't feel comfortable with.

We already implement something like this and we're a fantastically successful business. Why would we change what we know works?

This is what Julius Caesar might have said and look at what happened to the Roman Empire. What worked well in the past won't necessarily work in the future. The beauty of the RN Paradigm is that it is constantly adapting to fit new situations. If you make a decision and it turns out to be the wrong decision, the RN Paradigm will tell you that you should have done something different. If you make the right decision, then you can thank the paradigm and enjoy the fruits of success.

Like many other businesses, our management structures can be described using the standard Wilson-Vodolsky levels. How does the RN Paradigm fit into the standard WV system?

It would be absurd to construct a system of business management that doesn't conform to the seminal insights of the Wilson-Vodolsky system and I doubt there's a single successful business in operation today that isn't aware of their nine levels of leadership. The RN Paradigm is a complex and powerful strategy that is capable of steering any business through to success and as can be seen from diagram 21, the RN Paradigm is capable of generating level 6 management.

Diagram 21

For reference, the basic Wilson-Vodolsky management levels chart has been included.

The RN Paradigm

Level	Description
1 (Simple)	Tasks handed out at random to colleagues or passing strangers
2 (Tribal)	Coordinates tasks and assigns them to those with the appropriate skills or resources
3 (Feudal)	Delegates entire projects. Short-term plans (less than a year).
4 (Foundational)	Develops staff, understands the organisational structure as a whole. Two-year plans.
5 (Industrial)	Five-year plans, flourishing infrastructure, organic growth.
6 (Informational)	Removed from the quotidian. Visionary. Ten-year plans.
7 (Global)	Functions on behalf of the planet, aligns organisation with humanity's goals. Fifty-year plans.
8 (Cyber-technical)	Sublimation of the self, triumph over ego, actions are purely selfless. Hundred-year plans.
9 (Hyper-universal)	Navigates all conceivable possibilities, flawless comprehension, understands all employees. Leader defies description. Five-hundred-year plans.

Wilson-Vodolsky Management/leadership Levels

Andy R

We love the brilliant insights that the RN Paradigm makes, but obviously outsourcing our distribution hub deliverables on a bi-weekly mandated flow-rotator won't work, so what are we supposed to do? We have finite time and limited resources.

Your point about the RN Paradigm insights being brilliant is correct. Equally, you are wise to note that you have finite time and limited resources: so many businesses forget this. Implementing the paradigm won't necessarily solve your specific flow-rotator deliverables issue, but the paradigm will give you the far-sighted overview needed to recognize the structural components that may be producing the current shortfall in the quantization of your innovation-bubbles.

So, you're saying that businesses are best described, not by a single property, but by two properties: speed and aggression?

Yes.

Can the RN Paradigm predict the future and tell me what the most profitable market for my business is?

No.

How much time and effort will be needed from senior thought-visionaries to implement this system?

The RN Paradigm has been carefully designed to integrate seamlessly into the vast majority of existing leadership structures. The amount of time needed to adapt to its central insights and suggestions are likely to be negligible, with the possible exception of those tasked with implementing the new system, then it's likely to take up the entirety of their job for the remainder of their natural life.

I've read the book, but I found it somewhat incoherent: ideas were introduced, briefly discussed and then not taken any further. I'll be honest – it wasn't clear how we would go about implementing the paradigm in our organization.

This isn't phrased in the form of a question, but you do make an excellent point. However, we wouldn't expect you to understand the paradigm enough to implement it yourself any more than we would expect a high-school science student to solve the necessary equations for the successful functioning of a GPS satellite. The book is more of an introduction, it opens the door to a world of possible experience, like the first time you tried coffee or beer. Successful implementation of the RN Paradigm usually requires expensive presentations by our highly-trained staff, costly three-day training courses for your key-visionaries and high-end expert analysis of your organization by one of our elite RN-architects to establish the parameters for your specific business metric (SBM).

The RN Paradigm seems to spend very little time training managers in understanding themselves. Surely one must master the battle within before moving onto the external?

Of course and to some extent the paradigm identifies those individuals leading unexamined lives, but the paradigm does not seek to realign their self-awareness, it just identifies the need for that change to take place. The RN Paradigm is able to generate a two-dimensional dichotomy metric similar to that of the self/external knowledge of the Deacon Chart. However, the axes are more profound and the final chart is better represented with a five-dimensional plot.

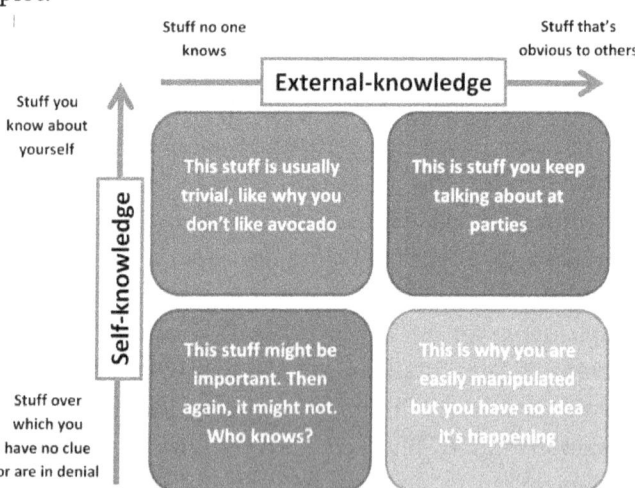

Deacon Chart (reproduced with the admiral's permission)

I have a friend who's a terrible manager. What's the best way for them to hold other people accountable for their questionable management strategies and problematic leadership skills?

One simple strategy is to be sufficiently chaotic that it becomes hard for people to know what you're working on at any one time. Dip in and out of projects, sometimes on an hourly or a monthly basis, stepping in, micromanaging stuff that's already been settled and then just moving onto something else without explaining why. In this way when a project fails you can spend time in meetings criticizing your own idiotic decisions by suggesting that these were decisions made by some subordinate and that despite you voicing your doubts at the time, you had decided to give them a chance. Your business will not improve, but your fragile ego will remain intact.

THE RN METRIC (SIMPLIFIED)

Sometimes it can be useful to have a rough idea of whether your team is more inclined towards speed or towards aggression and thus decide on how best to implement them. By identifying the types within your working group you can quickly and easily get a handle on whether you need to balance the group's dynamic, or whether to polarize the group further by enhancing its strongest assets.

The speed modulus (S) for a group is calculated by finding the average speed index for the group.

$$S = \frac{\sum_{i=1}^{N} s_i}{N\sqrt{2}}$$

The aggression modulus (A) is similarly calculated.

$$A = \frac{\sum_{i=1}^{N} a_i}{N\sqrt{2}}$$

The group quotient (Q) is then obtained by summing the squares of the aggression and speed moduli.

$$Q = \sqrt{S^2 + A^2}$$

This allows for the group's speed quotient to be calculated using:

$$S_Q = \frac{S}{Q}$$

And the group's aggression quotient to be calculated thus:

$$A_Q = \frac{A}{Q}$$

The speed quotient for a given organization can thus be calculated by expanding the previous expressions as follows:

$$= \frac{\left(\dfrac{S_1 + S_2 + S_3 + \cdots S_N}{N\sqrt{2}}\right)}{\sqrt{\left(\dfrac{S_1 + S_2 + S_3 + \cdots S_N}{N\sqrt{2}}\right)^2 + \left(\dfrac{A_1 + A_2 + A_3 + \cdots A_N}{N\sqrt{2}}\right)^2}}$$

The process looks a lot like taking the average and there is a good reason for this. The overall RN coefficient can be thus calculated using:

$$R_Q = \frac{S_Q}{A_Q}$$

If the R_Q is >1 then the group is Fast, if R_Q is <1 then the group is aggressive.

Armed with this simple numerical data we can thus start to analyze the efficacy of a working group with unprecedented and spurious precision. An example of this approach is contained in this book's appendix. Reading the appendix is neither required nor illuminating.

APPENDIX A

This appendix contains additional information on how the RN types can be employed to generate a single number with which you can completely and fully describe large groups of complex, multi-faceted individuals along with all of the interpersonal relationships they will develop.

A Hammer, two Tankers and a Grindstone; it sounds like a fun working group, but let's work out the total speed and aggression that they provide and summarize it in a table.

Immediately, we can see that this working group will be slow to adapt to change, but if they've been managed correctly, they will undertake their roles with a crushing amount of aggression.

The RN Paradigm

Type		Speed	Aggression
	Hammer	7.8	10.2
	Tanker	-8.0	11.2
	Tanker	-8.0	11.2
	Grindstone	0.752	6.82
Sum		-7.448	39.42

Let's employ the RN metric and get a more detailed understanding of how this group will function.

Let's take the speed component first. To calculate the speed modulus we take the sum of the speed and divide it by $4\sqrt{2}$ since there are four members of the working group.

This gives a speed modulus of

Andy R

$$S = \frac{10.52}{4\sqrt{2}} = -1.32$$

This is a low number because it is negative. The aggression modulus, similarly calculated, works out at A=+6.97. This is a positive number, which tells us it's greater than zero and that the aggression is high relative to the speed.

The group quotient (Q) is thus calculated at

$$Q = \sqrt{1.32^2 + 6.96^2} = 7.08$$

The group quotient (Q) gives us a good indication of the group's leverage within the organization. The theory underpinning the RN Paradigm is complex but simply put: the group quotient is an invariant quantity in economic space and thus remains constant under corporate transforms. Taking the entire staff and summing their quotient values tells us nothing useful, but it is an interesting exercise and it makes it look like you know what you're doing.

Here the group quotient is 7.08.

This is good. Or bad. It kind of depends on your perspective.

We use the invariant group quotient (Q) to calculate the relevant speed quotient (S_Q)

$$S_Q = \frac{-1.32}{7.08} = -0.19$$

Again, this is a low figure but to really get a sense of the group we also need a figure for the aggression quotient (A_Q) which works out at 0.967. These quotient values can fall between -1 and 1 and give a weighted sense of the group's dominant characteristic. A value of 0.967 suggests that this group is almost entirely about aggression.

The RN ratio calculates out 0.196. A balanced team will place a ratio around 1.0, but here we can see that the group is strongly positioned as your wrecking team.

Now you have a simple way to describe the whole group. You can walk onto the floor of any organization, be told the RN ratio of the working group is 0.196 and you will know everything you need to make a quick, ill-informed decision.

Whilst these single numbers are useful, it is also wise to examine the make-up of the group in more detail. Some aggressive groups work well in negotiations, particularly those with Thinkers on board, but this group would be far better suited to marketing.

The obvious downside to making team-build decisions using these abstracted numbers that are devoid of relevant personal information is it's likely to go horribly wrong. You're usually better off basing your choices on your knowledge of your team's personalities and then using these numbers to post-hoc rationalize your decision when the complaints start. People tend to be a bit scared of numbers and are much more likely to defer to a decision if you quote some number to a spurious precision. If you don't know enough about your team to make these types of decisions then your next step is clear: go and talk to them, get to know them and then make decisions and choices based on this information.

The RN Paradigm

If you enjoyed the RN Paradigm, you might enjoy an actual story by Andy R

ABOUT THE AUTHOR

Writing about yourself in the third person seems more than a little pompous and for someone who dislikes self-description, quite difficult. I'm curious, however, whether the author's post hoc autobiographical description would alter your perception of the preceding work? On some level, the preceding work is more of an insight into the author's mind than the curated facsimile they would seek to project here. I mean, at what point does the fiction end? If it helps: Andy R is a fantastically successful individual for whom all challenges are mere trifles and the blistering insights he offers are at their worst, enlightening and at their best, transcendent.

You could follow Andy R on twitter @AndyRwrites if that sort of thing appeals to you. It offers a slightly more pedestrian insight into his life, although, no less warped or curated.

Andy R

www.ingramcontent.com/pod-product-compliance
Lightning Source LLC
Chambersburg PA
CBHW070231180526
45158CB00001BA/389